MW01008460

Unless otherwise noted, all scriptural citations are from the
New King James Translations 1990, 1985, 1983, Thomas
Nelson, Nashville, Tn.

ISBN 978-1-937501-04-4 1-937501-04-3

Produced by
JaDon Management Inc.
1405 4th Ave. N. W. #109
Ardmore, Ok. 73401

Original Cover
by
Jeffrey T. McCormack
The Pendragon Web and Graphic Design
www.thependragon.net

2

FOREWORD

Revelation continues to be the source of endless prophetic speculation. Commentator after commentator tells us that the Apocalypse is about to happen! We are in the predicted "last days!"

Just this last year (2011) Harold Camping once again made world headlines with his prediction of the end of the world—but of course, nothing happened. There were literally parties around the world, sponsored by atheists, celebrating another failure on the part of those crazy Christians!

Of course, the sensationalistic predictions continue to fail, and will continue to fail, and provide the enemies of Christ more "ammunition" for their attacks on Christianity. It really is time for some sanity, some sound logic, some true exegesis to come to the fore and help put an end to the prophetic speculation.

Fueling many—if not most-- of the failed predictions of "the end" is a misguided view of the identity of Babylon of Revelation. We are told that Babylon is a restored literal Babylon in Iraq. She is New York City, or America. She is the Roman Catholic Church. We are told she is….well, you get the picture! The point is, that if you have the wrong identity of Babylon, you have a false eschatology. It is that simple.

In this relatively short work on the proper identity of the harlot city Babylon, Steve Temple brings a lot of what is needed to the table. His approach is solid, logical, textual and convincing.

Temple notes that Revelation exudes references to the Old Testament, insisting that to understand Revelation therefore, we must understand the prophecies that Revelation draws from. Eminently logical.

Building on the first point, Temple notes that the language of Revelation is taken directly from God's Old Covenant with Israel. This is a tremendously important and irrefutable point but, ignored by many commentators.

This leads to Temple's emphasis on Revelation being about the consummation of God's Covenant dealings with Israel, not the end of time or the end of the Christian age. Temple insists that Revelation is about Covenant Eschatology (the end of the Old Covenant) not "historical eschatology" i.e. the end of history. While he does not spend much time on it, Temple shows that all modern predictions of the end, based on Revelation, are in clear violation of the text, written 2000 years ago, that affirmed unequivocally that the end was near then.

A critical point in this work is Temple's demonstration that the very term "harlot" must be understood within the framework of an unfaithful bride, *a bride who has broken the marriage covenant*. This understanding of the word "harlot" demands a re-thinking of all traditional views of Revelation and eschatology. Lamentably, many, if not most commentators take the word "harlot" as having nothing to do with marital, i.e. covenant infidelity. This is a tremendous oversight.

Temple presents a wealth of evidence from the OT and God's dealings with Israel, demonstrating that the word harlot, indicated, not simply an immoral woman, but, *a wife who had become unfaithful*. This is *analogia scriptura* at its best!

With this understanding and definition established, there is only one city that can be identified as the Harlot of Revelation and that is Old Covenant Jerusalem, the Bride that had become unfaithful, shed innocent blood, and was about to be destroyed. Following that destruction, Christ would marry his bride, the righteous remnant of the twelve tribes (Revelation 7, 14) restored under and in her Messiah.

I am happy and honored to have a part in bringing this book to the reading public. This is a solid contribution to the literature, and will help all Bible students to face the future with confidence and assurance.

Don K. Preston D. Div.
President
Preterist Research Institute
www.eschatology.org   www.bibleprophecy.com

Who Was
The Mother of
Harlots?

By

Steve Temple

Contents:

A Look at the Book of Revelation

Introduction

Any discussion of "last things" that does not interact on a significant level with John's Apocalypse, must certainly be considered lacking to some degree. So much of modern eschatological teaching focuses on this writing, and I believe most modern interpretations miss the mark because of one basic hermeneutical flaw. This book filled with many fantastic images, has been subject to the vivid imaginations of numerous writers, many of whom were and are brilliant scholars. Since John's gospel differs markedly from the synoptic gospels in that it has no account of Jesus' Olivet Discourse, some have seen Revelation as John's version, only in expanded form. I believe that this is a very valid observation, because there are many parallels between John's work and our Lord's discourse found in Matthew 24 (see also Mark 13 and Luke 21). This perspective provides a very helpful point of reference for approaching this seemingly very complex tome.

Volume upon volume has been written speculating about and examining in minute detail the words and images found in this book. I have no intention of trying my hand at such a task. I don't have the ability or the interest at this time in trying to unravel all the intricacies of the book. In a sense, much of the detail is simply a matter of curiosity for us today. All of the details of this book may never be completely opened to our view. The book was directed specifically to a 1st century audience, and our being removed nearly two thousand years from the context presents us with many interpretive challenges and difficulties. Since I believe this book was speaking of events soon to take place (because that is what it repeatedly says), I also believe that it is not critical that we fully understand all the minutiae in order to benefit from and be impacted by the wonderfully powerful message imparted in this work.

Hermeneutic Keys

In this work I have refrained as much as possible from relying upon the opinions of others to make my arguments. I have tried to allow the scriptures to speak for themselves. The reader will have to decide for himself how successful I have been in this attempt. Nevertheless, I would like to share a brief comment from a work by Henry Hammond titled *A Premonition Concerning the Interpretation of the Apocalypse*, which was published in 1653. As Hammond began a project to review the translation of this final book of the New Testament, he was immediately confronted with the statement in the first verse, which spoke of things *"which must come to pass presently."* He found that these words "had such an impression on my mind, offering themselves as a key to the whole prophecy." He went on to say:

> "I could not resist the force of them, but attempted presently a general survey of the whole Book, to see whether those words might not probably be extended to all the prophecies of it, and have a literal truth in them, *viz.*, that the things foretold and represented in the ensuing vision; were *presently, speedily, to come to passe*, one after another, after the writing of them."

> "But before I could prudently passe this judgment, which was to be founded in ʼ

understanding the subject-matter of all the Visions, some other evidences I met with, concurring with this, and giving me abundant grounds of confidence of this one thing, that although I should not be able to understand one period of all these Visions, yet I must be obliged to think that they belonged to those times that were then immediately ensuing, and that they had accordingly their completion, and consequently that they that pretended to find in those Visions the predictions of events in these later ages, and those so nicely defined as to belong to particular acts and persons in this and some other kingdomes (a farre narrower curcuit also then that which resonably was to be assigned to that one Christian prophecie for the Universal Church of Christ) had much mistaken the drift of it."

In light of the above, my approach will be to look first at some of the temporal guidelines that clearly limit the scope of the material put forth in John's record. I would then like to address two closely linked issues. These are two of the primary themes addressed in Revelation, and I have found them to be tremendously compelling and helpful in attempting to determine the primary focus of the book. The first issue is the subject of the vindication of God's martyrs, and the second is the identity of the great city Babylon. There are an amazing number of theories and dogmatic teachings regarding the identity of Babylon that can easily confuse the student trying to properly understand this vision. The emphasis placed upon these topics in John's vision gives strong support to their centrality to the whole of the book of Revelation. Therefore if we can come to a better understanding of these two topics, we put ourselves in a much improved position to then understand how Jesus was to reveal (unveil) Himself through the events described in the book.

Dr. Don Preston has written an excellent book titled *Who Is This Babylon?* in which he deals with a much broader range of issues, examined in greater detail that pertain to this crucial question of the identity of Babylon. It may be obtained from his websites at www.eschatology.org and www.bibleprophecy.com/, as well as at Amazon.com. There are obviously many other works that address this issue; however, I highly recommend Preston's work as one that should be at the top of every list.

There is one crucial point that I would emphasize before moving on in the study. It must always be remembered when moving through this book, that it deals with God's promises to Israel. In Revelation 10, John told of seeing a mighty angel

16

holding an open book. When this angel cried out, *"seven thunders uttered their voices"* (v.3). Revelation 10:7 says: *"In the days of the sounding of the seventh angel, when he is about to sound, the mystery of God would be finished, as He declared to His servants the prophets."* Here it is said that the things written in this little book were related to the fulfillment of God's declarations to the prophets. These were Israel's prophets. It was they who had declared what became known in the New Testament as the mystery of God. It was this mystery that was also the focus of Paul's ministry. As the book of Acts closed, Paul informed the Jewish leaders in Rome: *"because for the hope of Israel I am bound with this chain"* (Acts 28:20).

Ultimately it must be understood that the mystery of God and the Hope of Israel were essentially one and the same. Paul was God's primary spokesman for revealing this wonderful mystery. It was plainly stated that throughout the entirety of his Christian ministry, he taught *"no other things than those which the prophets and Moses said would come"* (Acts 26:22). We must, therefore, see Revelation exclusively in the context of the fulfillment of God's promises to Israel. I think that this fact is essential to a proper understanding of Revelation.

From the very first verse of Revelation, God stated, in unambiguous language, that the things described within were events that must shortly take place. In Revelation 1:3, Jesus revealed that *"the time is near."* Later in verse 19 of chapter one, John was told: *"Write the things that thou hast seen, and the things that are, and the things that are about to come after those things"* (Young's Literal Translation). This verse very plainly speaks to things past, present, and of the immediate future (1ˢᵗ century context).

There is no indication whatsoever that Revelation deals with anything expected to happen in the far distant future. (I highly recommend Don K. Preston's special study of the millennium in his *Who Is this Babylon?* to support this claim).

In fact John presented multiple statements in the first chapter indicating that the forthcoming prophecy was to be fulfilled very soon. Nearing the end of the book and the conclusion of all the prophecies, statements in the final chapter only serve to strongly reinforce the statements of imminence presented in chapter 1. Revelation 22:6 repeats, almost verbatim, what was stated in Revelation 1:1. In Revelation 22:10 John was told not to *"seal the words of the prophecy of this book, for the time is at hand."* Finally, in Revelation 22:20 we find these closing words: *"The one who testifies to these things says, 'Yes, I am coming soon!' Amen! Come, Lord Jesus!"* (NET Bible). One must wonder how these statements could have been any more clear or emphatic. Why then are they so routinely and frequently ignored, disregarded, or explained away?

There are other passages that emphasize the temporal nearness of the events described in this book. They may not be as explicitly expressed; however, when properly understood they are certainly just as powerful. One such passage is found in Revelation 6 where we find Jesus opening the sixth seal. As the cosmic disturbances are revealed we find that,

> *"the kings of the earth, the great men, the rich men, the commanders, the mighty men, every slave and every free man, hid themselves in the caves and in the rocks of the mountains, and said to the mountains and rocks, 'Fall on us and hide us from the face of Him who sits on the throne and from the wrath of the Lamb!'"*
> (Revelation 6:15-16)

This is a direct quote from chapter 10 of Hosea's prophecy against Israel, in which God said: *"Ephraim shall receive shame, and Israel shall be ashamed of his own council. As for Samaria, her king is cut off like a twig on the water. Also the high places of Aven, the sin of Israel, shall be destroyed. The thorn and thistle shall grow on their altars; they shall say to the mountains, 'Cover us!' and to the hills, 'Fall on us!"* (Hosea 10:6-8).

It is important to note that Jesus quoted this same verse as He was being lead to the cross: *"And a great multitude of people followed Him, and women who also mourned and lamented Him. But Jesus, turning to them, said, 'Daughters of Jerusalem, do not weep for Me, but weep for yourselves and for your children. For indeed the days are coming in which they will say, 'Blessed are the barren, wombs that never bore, and breasts that never nursed!' Then they will begin 'to say to the mountains, 'Fall on us!' and to the hills, 'Cover us!''"* (Luke 23:27-30).

It is clear from Jesus' statement to *"weep for yourselves and for your children,"* that His expectation was that the terrible judgment pointed to in Hosea's prophecy would be fulfilled in that generation. Again, this simply serves to confirm and establish the time statements that bracket John's Apocalypse. There are other passages that could be cited, but they would simply be redundant because the sense of imminence found in this great book is already firmly established.

If the one investigating this revelation were to take these words seriously, it would give him a specific and limited context in which to begin and carry out his investigation. It would simplify the search for truth by placing upon it a specific time constraint. It would eliminate much of the varied and farfetched speculations commonly found in today's religious writings. By honoring these time parameters the searcher would be able to confine his studies to events contemporaneous to the writing of the book. In my view, this is the key hermeneutic that should guide any study of this book.

Shedding of Innocent Blood

The Apocalypse is literally saturated with quotes and images from, and allusions to, the Old Testament scriptures. An intimate knowledge and familiarity with these scriptures is, therefore, critical for a proper understanding of the book of Revelation. So much of what is found in these Old Covenant documents deals with God's covenant relationship with Israel. This critical observation seldom seems to hold the standing that it should when delving into the visions that John relays in the book of Revelation.

Throughout the Old Covenant writings, God went into great and emphatic detail regarding the consequences, for Israel, of covenant disobedience. A careful study of the language and images found in Revelation will shine light on the importance of passages such as Leviticus 26, Deuteronomy 28, and Deuteronomy 32.

Deuteronomy 28:59-60 says: *"If you do not carefully observe all the words of this law that are written in this book, that you may fear this glorious and awesome name, THE LORD YOUR GOD, then the LORD will bring upon you and your descendants extraordinary plagues—great and prolonged plagues—and serious and prolonged sicknesses. Moreover He will bring back on you all the diseases of Egypt, of which you were afraid, and they shall cling to you."* This in turn, pointed back to Exodus 7-12; chapters which are of critical importance for properly understanding much of what John saw in his Revelation.

One theme that stretches throughout the Bible is the vindication of God's martyrs. Genesis 4 presented the story of Cain and Abel. In verses 9 and 10, are these familiar words: *"Then the Lord said to Cain, 'Where is Abel your brother?' He said, 'I do not know. Am I my brother's keeper?' And He said, 'What have you done? The voice of your brother's blood cries out to Me from the ground."* Here is the story of the first martyr. He was called *"righteous Abel"* by Jesus in Matthew 23:35 and the writer of Hebrews listed Abel first in his great "hall of faith" in chapter 11.

The shedding of innocent blood continued as a major reason for God's condemnation of the nation of Israel. This is true throughout the remainder of the Old Testament and into the New. One of the most under appreciated passages for the typical Bible student (I know from personal experience) found anywhere in the Bible is Deuteronomy 32. In this amazing chapter, God announced how He would deal with Israel in her last days. At this point, Moses knew that his days were numbered and here was his final appeal to Israel to trust the God who had delivered them from bondage in Egypt. It was also an incredible prophecy of what would take place in Israel's last days.

Leading into the "Song of Moses," Moses lamented the certainty of Israel's future rebellion. *"For I know that after my death you will become utterly corrupt, and turn aside from the way which I have commanded you. And evil will befall you in the latter days, because you will do evil in the sight of the LORD, to provoke Him to anger through the work of your hands"* (Deuteronomy 31:29).

The Hebrew word translated here as "latter," is the same word (**achariyth**) translated in Genesis 49:1 as "last" in Jacob's prophecy to his children. (*"Gather together, that I may tell you what shall befall you in the last days"*). Twice in chapter 32, God used this word in describing things that would come upon His people. *"I will hide My face from them, I will see what their end (**achariyth**) will be, for they are a perverse generation, children in whom is no faith"* (Deuteronomy 32:20). Note here the English translation from the Greek Septuagint: "I will turn away my face from them, and will show what shall happen to them in the **last days**; for it is a perverse generation, sons in whom is no faith." Latter in verse 29, God said: *"Oh, that they were wise, that they understood this, that they would consider their latter (**achariyth**) end!"*

In this chapter, Moses set a pattern followed later by other Old Testament writers. He drew a distinction between God's people as Old Covenant Israel, and those identified as His servants (or in some passages, as His elect). It is imperative that we watch

24

closely the context of these passages. In some passages God may speak of "His people" in association with the whole nation of Israel, while in others there is a clear distinction made between His servants (elect) and those of Israel who were disobedient and who had rejected Him. Context is the key to determining how each phrase is to be understood. As Moses spoke of how God would judge Israel in their latter (last) days, he said:

> *"'Vengeance is Mine, and recompense; their* (Israel) *foot shall slip in due time; for the day of their* (Israel) *calamity is at hand, and the things to come hasten upon them* (Israel).' *'For the LORD will judge His people and have compassion on His servants, when He sees that their power is gone, and there is no one remaining, bond or free. . . . I will make My arrows drunk with blood, and My sword shall devour flesh, with the blood of the slain and the captives, from the heads of the leaders of the enemy.'' 'Rejoice, O Gentiles, with His people; for He will avenge the blood of His servants, and render vengeance to His adversaries; He will provide atonement for His land and His people'"*(Deuteronomy 32:35-36, 42-43). Parenthetical information mine – ST.

Here God stated that He would avenge the blood of His servants in Israel's latter (last) days. It is certainly important to note that in this passage God associated atonement for His people with the vengeance that would come against His enemies. That, however, is not the focus of our study at this point.

Israel's abysmal history of disobedience from the time of their entry into the promised land, is described for us from Joshua through 2 Chronicles. The service of the prophets Isaiah, Jeremiah and Ezekiel, covered the time frame when God dealt with Israel's unfaithfulness *and* came in judgment against both the Northern and the Southern kingdoms. Their prophecies were frequently interspersed with words condemning Israel for shedding innocent blood.

In the first chapter of Isaiah's prophecy, he made it perfectly clear that his vision concerned Judah and Jerusalem. *"The vision of Isaiah the son of Amoz, which he saw concerning Judah and Jerusalem"* (Isaiah 1:1). Later in that chapter God said: *"Your New Moons and your appointed feasts My soul hates; they are a trouble to Me, I am weary of bearing them. When you spread out your hands, I will hide My eyes from you; even though you make many prayers, I will not hear. Your hands are full of blood."* (Isaiah 1:14-15).

God would not hear their prayers because of the blood that they had shed. In chapter 4, Isaiah pointed to a time, *"When the Lord has washed away the filth of the daughters of Zion, and purged the blood of Jerusalem from her midst, by the spirit of judgment and by the spirit of burning"* (Isaiah 4:4).

Chapter 59 brought even more scathing words from God. *"But your iniquities have separated you from your God; and your sins have hidden His face from you, so that He will not hear. For your hands are defiled with blood"* (Isaiah 59:2-3). He said: *"Their webs will not become garments, nor will they cover themselves with their works; their works are works of iniquity, and the act of violence is in their hands. Their feet run to evil, and they make haste to shed innocent blood; their thoughts are thoughts of iniquity; wasting and destruction are in their paths"* (Isaiah 59:6-7).

It was obvious from Isaiah's prophecy that God would hold Israel accountable for the unjust shedding of blood. It is equally clear from Isaiah 4:4 that God would wash away the filth of the daughters of Zion and purge the blood of Jerusalem by the spirit of judgment and burning. Israel's salvation would come about through and be associated with judgment.

God's judgment had already come upon the Northern tribes when He called Jeremiah to prophecy to Judah and Jerusalem. In chapter 2, there is a familiar message: *"Why do you beautify your way to seek love? Therefore you have also taught the wicked women your ways. Also on your skirts is found the blood of the lives of the poor innocents"* (Jeremiah 2:33-34). In chapter 19, Jeremiah said: *"Hear the word of the LORD, O kings of Judah and inhabitants of Jerusalem. Thus says the LORD of hosts, the God of Israel: "Behold, I will bring such a catastrophe on this place, that whoever hears of it, his ears will tingle. "Because they have forsaken Me and made this an alien place, because they have burned incense in it to other gods whom neither they, their fathers, nor the kings of Judah have known, and have filled this place with the blood of the innocents"* (Jeremiah 19:3-4). In chapter 22, God contrasted the righteous rein of Josiah with that of his son Shallum. *"He judged the cause of the poor and needy; then it was well. Was not this knowing Me?" says the LORD. "Yet your eyes and your heart are for nothing but your covetousness, for shedding innocent blood, and practicing oppression and violence"* (Jeremiah 22:16-17).

Jeremiah lived through the Babylonian siege of Jerusalem and witnessed the subsequent destruction of the temple and the city. He recognized that the devastation and destruction was a judgment from God. He said:

> *"The LORD has fulfilled His fury, He has poured out His fierce anger. He kindled a fire in Zion, and it has devoured its foundations. The*

kings of the earth, and all inhabitants of the world, would not have believed that the adversary and the enemy could enter the gates of Jerusalem— because of the sins of her prophets and the iniquities of her priests, who shed in her midst the blood of the just. They wandered blind in the streets; they have defiled themselves with blood, so that no one would touch their garments " (Lamentations 4:11- 14).

Here again it is confirmed that the focus of God's judgment of Jerusalem and Judah was a result in large part to the shedding of innocent blood.

Ezekiel was a contemporary of Jeremiah and dealt with many of the same issues. Through him God warned Israel of imminent judgment and in chapter 7 said: *"I will turn My face from them, and they will defile My secret place; for robbers shall enter it and defile it. 'Make a chain, for the land is filled with crimes of blood, and the city is full of violence'"* (Ezekiel 7:22-23).

Ezekiel 16 is likewise a devastating account of Jerusalem's unfaithfulness to their God. We will spend considerably more time with that chapter later, but for now note these words:

"'Now then, O harlot (Jerusalem), *hear the word of the LORD! Thus says the Lord GOD: 'Because your filthiness was poured out and your nakedness uncovered in your harlotry with your lovers, and with all your abominable idols, and because of the blood of your children which you gave to them, surely, therefore, I will gather all your lovers with whom you took pleasure, all those you loved, and all those you hated; I will gather them from all around against you and will uncover your nakedness to them, that they may see all your nakedness'"* (Ezekiel 16:35-37).

Chapters 22 and 23 continued this theme with Ezekiel listing the sins of Jerusalem and then describing in chapter 23 Israel and Judah as two harlot sisters. He began chapter 22 with these unsettling words:

"Now, son of man, will you judge, will you judge the bloody city? Yes, show her all her abominations! Then say, 'Thus says the Lord GOD: 'The city sheds blood in her own midst, that her time may come; and she makes idols within herself to defile herself. You have become guilty by the blood which you have shed, and have defiled yourself with the idols which you

have made. You have caused your days to draw near, and have come to the end of your years; therefore I have made you a reproach to the nations, and a mockery to all countries. Those near and those far from you will mock you as infamous and full of tumult. 'Look, the princes of Israel: each one has used his power to shed blood in you'" (Ezekiel 22:2-6).

The Lord here identified Jerusalem as "the bloody city." This characterization by God of the supposed "holy city" should be placed in the forefront of our minds as we make our way to examine the New Testament and more particularly as we seek to identify Babylon of Revelation.

The prophet continued in this vein and had more of the same for the harlot sisters. *"The LORD also said to me: "Son of man, will you judge Oholah and Oholibah? Then declare to them their abominations. For they have committed adultery, and blood is on their hands. They have committed adultery with their idols, and even sacrificed their sons whom they bore to Me, passing them through the fire, to devour them"* (vv.36-37).

Near the end of Ezekiel's prophecy, we find God's promise to restore Israel (the Northern tribes). However, before describing the renewal, he recounted the reasons for their present condition of exile from their land.

31

"Moreover the word of the LORD came to me, saying: 'Son of man, when the house of Israel dwelt in their own land, they defiled it by their own ways and deeds; to Me their way was like the uncleanness of a woman in her customary impurity. Therefore I poured out My fury on them for the blood they had shed on the land, and for their idols with which they had defiled it. So I scattered them among the nations, and they were dispersed throughout the countries; I judged them according to their ways and their deeds'" (Ezekiel 36:16-19).

As we move on to Hosea, it should be recognized that he was used by God in a very unique and remarkable way. His life was a living parable to Israel in which God promised horrible judgment, but there was also a promise of restoration to a people who because of their unfaithfulness were to be cast among the nations. These were the people of whom He said, *"In the place where it was said to them, 'You are not My people,' there it shall be said to them, ' You are sons of the living God'"* (Hosea 1:10). His prophecy was addressed to Israel in the years immediately preceding the Assyrian advance on the Northern kingdom. In chapter 1, God told Hosea: *"I will avenge the bloodshed of Jezreel on the house of Jehu, and bring an end to the kingdom of the house of Israel"* (v.4).

Gilead was described in chapter 6 as, *"a city of evildoers and defiled with blood"* (v.8).

We could review the historical writings of the Old Testament and find numerous specific examples of Israel's transgressions in killing the innocent; however, the preceding discussion should make it abundantly clear that Israel's history in this regard was a prime reason for the promised judgment that was to come upon Israel and Judah. Clearly God judged His peoples through the instrumentality of the Assyrians in 722BC and the Babylonians in 586BC. As noted above, Jeremiah, who lived on this side of the Babylonian destruction of Jerusalem, noted that this judgment had been in response to the shedding of innocent blood (Lamentations 4). God promised Jeremiah that He would restore Jerusalem after 70 years of captivity, but He also gave Daniel a vision of His consummative purposes for finally dealing with Old Covenant Israel.

Daniel Chapter 9:24-27:

> *"Seventy weeks are determined for your people and for your holy city, to finish the transgression, to make an end of sins, to make reconciliation for iniquity, to bring in everlasting righteousness, to seal up vision and prophecy, and to anoint the Most Holy. 'Know therefore and understand, that from the going*

forth of the command to restore and build Jerusalem until Messiah the Prince, there shall be seven weeks and sixty-two weeks; the street shall be built again, and the wall, even in troublesome times. 'And after the sixty-two weeks Messiah shall be cut off, but not for Himself; and the people of the prince who is to come shall destroy the city and the sanctuary. The end of it shall be with a flood, and till the end of the war desolations are determined. Then he shall confirm a covenant with many for one week; but in the middle of the week He shall bring an end to sacrifice and offering, and on the wing of abominations shall be one who makes desolate, even until the consummation, which is determined, is poured out on the desolate.'"

3½ yrs

This passage is pivotal. There is much disagreement over its interpretation among "conservative" Christian scholars. In this section, Daniel was told that *"seventy weeks are determined for your people* (Israel) *and for the holy city"* (Daniel 9:24). This included God's promise to Jeremiah to *"restore and build Jerusalem"* (Daniel 9:25). He was told that during those seventy weeks, Israel would finish the transgression and that *"the people of the prince who is to come shall destroy the city and the sanctuary"* (Daniel 9:26).

34

In Matthew 23:32, Jesus seemed to be referring specifically to this passage in Daniel as He spoke to the Jewish leaders. He said to them, *"Fill up the measure of your fathers' guilt."* How is it that they would do this? Jesus said: *"Indeed, I send you prophets, wise men, and scribes: some of them you will kill and crucify, and some of them you will scourge in your synagogues and persecute from city to city"* (Matthew 23:34).

As a result of this persecution, Jesus said *"that on you* (the 1st century Jewish leaders) *may come all the righteous blood shed on the earth, from the blood of righteous Abel to the blood of Zechariah, son of Berechiah, whom you murdered between the temple and the altar. Assuredly, I say to you, all these things will come upon this generation"* (Matthew 23:35-36). It is widely acknowledged that this prediction by Jesus was in reference to the destruction of Jerusalem in 70AD.

Daniel was next told that, *"the end of it shall be with a flood, and till the end of the war desolations are determined"* (Daniel 9:26). The prophet was told that *within those seventy weeks* the city Jerusalem and its sanctuary would be rebuilt, but that at the end they would become desolate when they were destroyed by the people of the prince who was to come. When Jesus' generation filled up the measure of their fathers' guilt (finished transgression), the end would come. The end of what?

When Gabriel said, *"the end of it will come with a flood,"* he was no doubt referring to the Roman desolation of Jerusalem and the surrounding lands. There is nothing in the context here that would lead us to believe that the "end" Gabriel mentioned is the end of time or the physical creation. He was pointing to the destruction of the city and sanctuary at which time God's purpose, *"to make an end of sins, to make reconciliation for iniquity, to bring in everlasting righteousness, to seal up vision and prophecy, and to anoint the Most Holy"* (Daniel 9:24) would be fulfilled.

Israel's salvation would be consummated at the time of her judgment. Those who received Israel's Messiah and His New Covenant, received their salvation when the Christ appeared a second time for salvation (Hebrews 9:28). This occurred simultaneously with His coming in judgment to destroy the last vestiges of the Old Covenant system and to vindicate the true martyrs of God. We can now see that Daniel's prophesy ties in directly to this overarching theme of martyr vindication found all the way through the Bible. As we will see this is a theme of particular importance in the book of Revelation.

Many today speak of the end of the world and the end of time as Biblically derived doctrines, and yet nowhere in the Scriptures do we find any mention of the end of time or the physical creation. In a number of places we find reference to an end, or the "time of the end," but nowhere does it speak of the end of time. There are certainly those passages, noted earlier, in the King James Version, that are translated "end of the world" (see Matthew 13:39, 40, 49; Matthew 28:20). We have demonstrated, however, that these refer to the end of Israel's Old Covenant age, rather than the physical creation.

Daniel in particular used the phrase "the time of the end" several times. After being given further details about things that would happen to Israel in its future, Daniel was told: *"Shut up the words, and seal the book until the time of the end"* (Daniel 12:4). Just a few verses later, he was again told: *"Go your way, Daniel, for the words are closed up and sealed till the time of the end"* (Daniel 12:9). When he asked: *"How long shall the fulfillment of these wonders be?"* he was told: *"When the power of the holy people has been completely shattered, all these things shall be finished"* (Daniel 12:8). Israel was the only people ever designated as holy, or set apart to God. This was surely a reference to the destruction of the symbol of Old Covenant Israel's power when the Temple *and* the "holy city" fell under the judgment of their Messiah through the hands of the Roman armies. That was to be, not the end of time, but the time of the end.

Daniel was also told in Daniel 12:2 (*"And many of those who sleep in the dust of the earth shall awake, some to everlasting life. Some to shame and everlasting contempt"*) as well as in the last verse of the prophecy (*"But you, go your way till the end; for you shall rest, and will arise to your inheritance at the end of the days"* Daniel 12:13), that the resurrection would take place *"at the end of the days."* Notice that it was not to be the end of days such as we might say in regard to the end of time or the end of human history. This was in reference to the end of the seventy week period, and it should again point us back to the things that would be fulfilled at the destruction of Jerusalem when, *"the power of the holy people was completely shattered."*

As we have noted previously, in the closing chapter of his revelation, John was told: *"Do not seal up the words of the prophecy of this book, for the time is at hand"* (Revelation 22:10). It is safe to say that most biblical scholars believe that Revelation is largely about the fulfillment of Daniel's prophecy. In Revelation chapter five, we are introduced to, *"a scroll written inside and on the back, sealed with seven seals"* (Revelation 5:1). The only One worthy to open this scroll was the Lion of the tribe of Judah, the Root of David, none other than Jesus Christ the Son of God. He had, *"prevailed to open the scroll and to loose its seven seals"* (Revelation 5:5). As He opened the seals, the Lamb of God was revealing the events of the prophecy which according to first verse of chapter 1, as well as verse 6 of chapter 22, *"must shortly take place."* The "time" that John was told was "at hand," was Daniel's "time of the end."

38

One of the climatic events described in Revelation was the destruction of the harlot city Babylon the Great, who was, *"drunk with the blood of the saints and with the blood of the martyrs of Jesus"* (17:6). She was the city in whom was, *"found the blood of the prophets and saints, and of all who were on the earth"* (18:24). At the fall of Babylon the angel exhorted: *"Rejoice over her, O heaven, and you holy apostles and prophets, for God has avenged you on her!"* (18:20).

In the first verses of chapter 19, these powerful words clearly reveal the supreme importance of what had taken place at the fall of the harlot city: *"After these things I heard a loud voice of a great multitude in heaven, saying, 'Alleluia! Salvation and glory and honor and power belong to the Lord our God! For true and righteous are His judgments, because He has judged the great harlot who corrupted the earth with her fornication; and He has avenged on her the blood of His servants shed by her'"* (vv.1-2).

Jesus had stated as plainly as possible in Matthew 23 who He held responsible for *"all the righteous blood shed on the earth"* (v.35). Likewise, in Luke 13, He told the Pharisees: *"It cannot be that a prophet should perish outside of Jerusalem. 'O Jerusalem, Jerusalem, the one who kills the prophets and stones those who are sent to her!"* (vv.33-34). It seems to me that the connection established here between Old Covenant

Jerusalem and Babylon the great of Revelation is established beyond any possible contradiction.

It is difficult to overemphasize that Jesus told the Jewish leaders that He held them responsible for, *"all the righteous blood shed on the earth,"* and that, *"all these things will come upon this* (1ˢᵗ century) *generation"* (Matthew 23:36). The importance of these statements just cannot be ignored.

In His parable of the persistent widow Jesus compared the actions of the unjust judge with those of His Father. *"Then the Lord said, 'Hear what the unjust judge said. And shall not God avenge His own elect who cry out day and night to Him, though He bears long with them? I tell you that He will avenge them speedily"* (Luke 18:6-7). The Greek word **tachos** translated here as "speedily" is more often translated as "shortly," and always (even when translated as "speedily") indicates a sense of imminence rather than simple speed or rapidity of action.

There is a parallel in Revelation that reinforces God's intent to avenge His saints in short order. *"When He opened the fifth seal, I saw under the altar the souls of those who had been slain for the word of God and for the testimony which they held. And they cried with a loud voice saying, 'How long, O Lord, holy and true, until You judge and avenge our blood on those who dwell on the earth?' Then a white robe was given to each of them; and it was said to them that they should rest a*

blood drains under altar

40

little while longer, until both the number of their fellow servants and their brethren, who would be killed as they were, was completed" (6:6-11). This passage asserts that God would avenge the blood of the martyrs in "a little while." It is in complete agreement with Jesus' prophecy in Matthew 23:34 that the Jews would kill, crucify, scourge and persecute the prophets, wise men, and scribes that He would send them. When the killing was complete, when they had filled up the measure of their Fathers' guilt, then as Jesus plainly stated, judgment would come upon that generation.

We have followed this theme from the opening chapters of Genesis through to this last great prophecy. It should now be firmly established that the vindication of all the righteous blood shed on the earth that Jesus said would come against that generation, is what is being portrayed in the graphic language and images used by John to describe the utter destruction of Babylon the great. From a scriptural perspective, it stands that the harlot city really could be none other than Old Covenant Jerusalem.

As I have noted earlier, it is common for many modern day Christians to diminish the importance of what took place in the fall of Jerusalem in 70AD. Some have stated that there is essentially no theological significance associated with these events. If what we have established here regarding the correspondence between Babylon of Revelation and Old

41

Covenant Jerusalem is indeed true, however, this view is in distinct disagreement with the claims of Scripture.

In chapter 18, John reaffirmed the finality of Babylon's fall and then began chapter 19 (some of which I have already quoted) by describing a scene of great exultation in heaven in response to the demise of the great harlot:

> *"After these things I heard a loud voice of a great multitude in heaven, saying, 'Alleluia! Salvation and glory and honor and power belong to the Lord our God! For true and righteous are His judgments, because He has judged the great harlot who corrupted the earth with her fornication; and He has avenged on her the blood of His servants shed by her.' Again they said, 'Alleluia! Her smoke rises up forever and ever!' And the twenty-four elders and the four living creatures fell down and worshiped God who sat on the throne, saying, 'Amen! Alleluia!' Then a voice came from the throne, saying, 'Praise our God, all you His servants and those who fear Him, both small and great!' And I heard, as it were, the voice of a great multitude, as the sound of many waters and as the sound of mighty thunderings, saying, 'Alleluia! For the Lord God Omnipotent reigns!*

*Let us be glad and rejoice and give Him glory,
for the marriage of the Lamb has come, and His
wife has made herself ready.' And to her it was
granted to be arrayed in fine linen, clean and
bright, for the fine linen is the righteous acts of
the saints"* (Revelation 19:1-8).

church is Bride of Christ

According to this passage, God's faithfulness was confirmed in a very powerful way as He avenged the blood of His servants. Not only this, but the culmination of Babylon's destruction led directly to the marriage of the Lamb, just as depicted in Jesus' parable of the Wedding Feast in Matthew 22:1-14.

Not all that was accomplished during this epic time in the history of Israel was discernable by the natural senses. Indeed the events of the war were in large part signs of spiritual events that resulted in theological/covenantal changes of insuperable importance. Within the imagery of the marriage of the Lamb, we find the final consummation of the New Covenant that God had promised to make with Israel and Judah.

The Mother of Harlots

As we move on, we find that there are several charges imbedded in the titles given her (aside from her complicity in the killing of God's saints and the martyrs of Jesus) that can aid us in our efforts to positively identify this Babylon. In Revelation chapter 17, one of the seven angels carried John away in the Spirit into the wilderness. Here he,

> *"saw a woman sitting on a scarlet beast which was full of names of blasphemy, having seven heads and ten horns. The woman was arrayed in purple and scarlet, and adorned with gold and precious stones and pearls, having in her hand a golden cup full of abominations and the filthiness of her fornication. And on her forehead a name was written: MYSTERY, BABYLON THE GREAT, THE MOTHER OF HARLOTS AND OF THE ABOMINATIONS OF THE EARTH." I saw the woman, drunk with the blood of the saints and with the blood of the martyrs of Jesus. And when I saw her, I marveled with great amazement* (Revelation 17:3-6).

If we allow the Old Testament scriptures to guide and inform us we will see that this graphic description of Babylon the great

44

found in Revelation, pointed to none other than 1st century Jerusalem, as representative of Old Covenant Judaism.

As is so often the case, the Old Testament is the key to a proper understanding of most if not all of the images used in the New Testament. We see that Babylon is referred to as *"the mother of harlots, and of the abominations of the earth."* These two terms – "harlotry" and "abominations"- are used almost exclusively in the Old Testament in reference to Israel, Judah and Jerusalem. No other people are accused of committing harlotries. This is primarily because no other people shared the favored status and relationship that Israel had with Jehovah. Israel was God's covenant people. He had married them (Jeremiah 31:32) and as such Israel was central to God's redemptive purposes that would ultimately reach out to all nations.

It is puzzling that some very learned scholars insist that the use of the Greek word **Porne** in this context precludes the possibility of covenant relationship, whether it be Israel (Jesusalem) or the Roman Church.

In his discussion of the harlot of Revelation, Tom Holland points to William Hendriksen's commentary on Revelation and states the following: "He has pointed out that the description used by John is not *an adulteress* – as the reformers' interpretation of the Roman Church having forsaken the covenant would require – but a harlot having no covenant with Yahweh" (*Contours of Pauline Theology*, p.131). Footnote no.3 on p. 167 of Hendriksen's book *More Than Conquerors,* says this: "Babylon is never called *moichalis,* 'adulteress'; always *porne,* 'harlot.' Hence, Babylon was never the Lamb's wife."

Both these men are contending that the term *harlot* cannot be used in a covenantal (or marriage) context. Yet, they then apply this language to some theoretical covenant that the Roman Catholic Church forsook. But, if the language can apply to the Catholic church, ostensibly violating her (non-existent) covenant, then why would that language not apply to God's covenantal relationship with Israel as well?

In my mind, this is a truly remarkable proposition. In essence these scholars have totally rejected the Old Testament foundation that is the key to developing a proper biblical understanding of the New Testament usage of this concept of harlotry. The Old Testament is replete with warnings against, as well as actual charges of harlotry. Significantly, all these charges were made in relationship to God's covenant people.

Israel's covenant relationship was the whole basis for the use of this imagery. It was used in response to her unfaithfulness to Yahweh, her husband. From a biblical perspective, a legitimate charge of harlotry can only be made against His covenant people. As will be seen shortly, there are several passages that clearly link harlotry and adultery and show that they are synonymous concepts in the minds of God and His prophets. There is no biblical justification whatsoever for dissociating the concept of harlotry from covenant relationship. This is a crucial point upon which these scholars clearly misrepresent the Old Testament texts and therefore mislead their readers.

Since these terms figure prominently in a number of Old Testament passages, it is then from the Old Testament that the biblical context of these concepts and terms must be established. Certainly, most have a reasonable understanding of the modern concept of harlotry. Perhaps the same could also be said regarding the basic principle behind the term abomination. We must, however, determine whether these terms are simply used in a general way, or if instead they are found within a specific context. Hopefully no one familiar with the scriptures would deny the assertion that the Old Testament deals primarily with God's relationship with a people called Israel. Very early in these writings, God revealed His intention to take for Himself a special people who would be set apart from the other nations, but through whom His blessings would flow to the other nations. This began with His calling of Abram and the subsequent covenant promises that God made to him (Genesis 12:3) that through him all the nations of the earth would be blessed.

Having brought Israel out of Egypt and through the Red Sea, God gave Moses the Ten Commandments as Israel's covenant document. These are recorded in Exodus 20. In the chapters that immediately follow (Exodus 21-23), Israel was given additional laws and commandments. At the end of chapter 23, God specifically stated that Israel should make no covenants with the people that He was about to drive out of the land. He said, *"You shall make no covenant with them, nor with their gods. They shall not dwell in your land, lest they make you sin against Me. For if you serve their gods, it will surely be a snare to you"* (Exodus 23:32-33). Chapter 24:3 said: *"Moses came and told the people all the words of the Lord and all the judgments. And all the people answered with one voice and said, 'All the words which the Lord has said we will do.'"*

Sometime later, God told Moses: *"Speak to the children of Israel: Tell them to make tassels on the corners of their garments throughout their generations, and to put a blue thread in the tassels of the corner. And you shall have the tassel, that you may look upon it and remember all the commandments of the LORD and do them, and that you may not follow the harlotry to which your own heart and your own eyes are inclined, and that you may remember and do all My commandments, and be holy for your God"* (Numbers 15:38-40). Clearly harlotry is here directly associated with Israel's covenant relationship with Yahweh. With good reason, God

48

continued to warn these people to be faithful to Him or realize that they would *"surely perish"* (Deuteronomy 8:19).

Despite their continual rebellion (as chronicled in Deuteronomy 9), God steadfastly emphasized His particular love for His covenant people: *"For you are a holy people to the LORD your God; the LORD your God has chosen you to be a people for Himself, a special treasure above all the peoples on the face of the earth. The LORD did not set His love on you nor choose you because you were more in number than any other people, for you were the least of all peoples; but because the LORD loves you, and because He would keep the oath which He swore to your fathers, the LORD has brought you out with a mighty hand, and redeemed you from the house of bondage, from the hand of Pharaoh king of Egypt"* (Deuteronomy 7:6-8).

Clearly God had expectations of Israel that He had placed upon no other peoples. Israel had wonderful privileges (see Romans 9:4-5), as well as promised blessings as a result of this special relationship. All these would come as a result of her faithfulness to her Husband. Just as it is with any husband who marries the love of his life, God had promised to provide for Israel's every need, and to do so with great and bountiful blessings. Not to be overlooked, however, faithfulness was the expected response from the one receiving these blessings. In fact, God's blessings were conditioned solely upon that response (Exodus 19:5; Deuteronomy 26:17-19).

With the time of Moses' death quickly approaching, the LORD spoke to him and said: *"Behold, you will rest with your fathers; and this people will rise and play the harlot with the gods of the foreigners of the land, where they go to be among them, and they will forsake Me and break my covenant which I have made with them"* (Deuteronomy 31:16). The words of this prophecy were confirmed repeatedly throughout Israel's history. Despite the centuries of despicable behavior, as portrayed in Hosea's living parable, the prophets of God continued to express His "heartfelt" love for Israel.

In the 43rd chapter of Isaiah's prophecy, God identified Himself as Israel's Redeemer. In this passage He reasserted His love for her.

> *"But now, thus says the LORD, who created you, O Jacob, and He who formed you, O Israel: 'Fear not, for I have redeemed you; I have called you by your name; you are Mine. When you pass through the waters, I will be with you; and through the rivers, they shall not overflow you. When you walk through the fire, you shall not be burned, nor shall the flames scorch you. For I am the LORD your God, the Holy One of*

Israel, your Savior; I gave Egypt for your ransom, Ethiopia and Seba in your place. Since you were precious in My sight, you have been honored, and I have loved you, therefore I will give men for you, and people for your life'"
(Isaiah 43:1-4).

How richly beautiful are these words of love, made even to a rebellious people who were never able to fully live up to the words of their ancestors: *"All the words which the Lord has said we will do"* (Exodus 24:3).

In Jeremiah 31, the prophet spoke of the true people of God (*"O LORD, save Your people, the remnant of Israel"* Jeremiah 31:7). This wonderful chapter is where He promised to make a New Covenant with the houses of Israel and Judah. The Lord began with these words of comfort: *"'At that same time* ("the latter, or last days" when He would restore Israel; Jeremiah 30:24)*' says the LORD, 'I will be the God of all the families of Israel, and they shall be My people.' Thus says the LORD: 'The people who survived the sword found grace in the wilderness – Israel, when I went to give him rest.' The LORD has appeared of old to me, saying: 'Yes, I have loved you with an everlasting love; therefore with lovingkindness I have drawn you. Again I will build you, and you shall be rebuilt, O virgin of Israel! You shall again be adorned with your tambourines, and shall go forth in the dances of those who rejoice"* (Jeremiah 31:1-4). Here God was committing Himself to restore the true Israel – the faithful remnant (see Isaiah 10:20-22; 11:11-16). Nevertheless, this was a remarkable expression of His unconditional love for His covenant people.

The Old Testament closes with a final affirmation of God's special, particular love for Israel: *"The burden of the word of the LORD to Israel by Malachi. 'I have loved you,' says the LORD. 'Yet you say, 'In what way have You loved us?' Was not Esau Jacob's brother?' says the LORD. 'Yet Jacob I have loved; but Esau I have hated, and laid waste his mountains and his heritage for the jackals of the wilderness'"* (Malachi 1:1-3).

Here again it is clear that God's love for Israel was unique – it was as a husband's love for his wife. (*"For your Maker is your husband, The LORD of hosts is His name; And your Redeemer is the Holy One of Israel; He is called the God of the whole earth"* Isaiah 54:5) It was exclusive and with it came the expectation of a faithful love in return. Anytime Israel looked to anyone or anything other than Yahweh, she was in essence turning to other lovers. This is the context of God's relationship with Israel that we must always keep before us in our investigation of all of Scripture, but in particular at this juncture of our study, the book of Revelation.

It was in the context of this exclusive covenant (marriage) relationship that the Old Testament writers use such terms as harlotry, unfaithfulness, fornication and abominations. It was why God condemned Israel for chasing after other lovers. We find this terminology employed throughout the historical, as well as the prophetic writings.

In the "last days" prophecy of Deuteronomy 32, God spoke of what would happen to Israel in her latter days (Deuteronomy 31:29). *"They have provoked Me to jealousy by what is not God; they have moved Me to anger by their foolish idols. But I will provoke them to jealousy by those who are not a nation; I will move them to anger by a foolish nation"* (Deuteronomy 32:21). This was language reflecting a covenant/marriage relationship in which jealousy was aroused through unfaithfulness. Note that this passage was quoted by Paul in Romans 10:19 as being fulfilled through his ministry to the Gentiles in the 1st century. Nowhere do we ever find God expressing Himself in this manner regarding any people other than Israel.

In the next few pages, a representative sampling will be given of the multitude of passages that could be cited showing that the titles assigned to Babylon the great are terms frequently used to describe the character (or lack thereof) and actions of God's covenant people, both before and after the kingdom was divided. The titles are terms that only have relevance in the context of an intimate relationship between God and His people Israel. They have no real Biblical significance outside the context of this covenant. Throughout the Old Testament God expressed His grief, anger, frustration, jealousy, etc. over the unfaithfulness of His chosen people.

Keep in mind that we see something directly analogous when Jesus spoke to the scribes, Pharisees, and Sadducees and said: *"An evil and adulterous generation seeks after a sign"* (Matthew 12:39; see also 16:4 and Mark 8:38). We can properly understand His reference to an "adulterous generation," only in the context of Judah's covenant relationship with God.

The Greek word **moichalis** here translated as "adulterous" is defined in The KJV New Testament Greek Lexicon (found at www.bible.crosswalk.com) as follows: "As the intimate alliance of God with the people of Israel was likened to a marriage, those who relapse into idolatry are said to commit adultery or play the harlot; a. figuratively equivalent to faithless to God, unclean, apostate." Similarly, when we find James lashing out at those who were filled with pride and who had caused strife within the church, he used essentially the same imagery. *"Adulterers and adulteresses! Do you not know that friendship with the world is enmity with God? Whoever therefore wants to be a friend of the world makes himself an enemy of God"* (James 4:4).

The same Greek word is this time translated as "adulterers" and "adulteresses." James clearly identified them as enemies of God, in contrast to those who humble themselves in obedience before Him - those who God said He would lift up (James 4:10). Jesus and His brother James addressed the same issues as the Old Testament prophets had in their messages of warning to Old Covenant Israel. The major difference is that Jesus and James were not looking hundreds of years into the future, but were specifically addressing the people to whom Jesus said: *"All these things will come upon this generation"* (Matthew 23:36).

At the time of Israel's beginnings as a covenant nation, God was prepared to give Moses the Ten Commandments and this is what He said: *"Now therefore, if you will indeed obey My voice and keep My covenant, then you shall be a special treasure to Me above all people; for all the earth is Mine"* (Exodus 19:5). In Deuteronomy 7:6-8, God described His choosing of Israel. This established the foundation of His commitment to them.

> *"For you are a holy people to the LORD your God; the LORD your God has chosen you to be a people for Himself, a special treasure above all the peoples on the face of the earth. The LORD did not set His love on you nor choose you because you were more in number than any*

other people, for you were the least of all people, but because the LORD loves you and because He would keep the oath which He swore to your fathers, the LORD has brought you out with a mighty hand, and redeemed you from the house of bondage, from the hand of Pharaoh king of Egypt."

As the forty years of wilderness wandering drew to a close, God spoke through Moses and prepared the wilderness generation for their entry into the Promised Land. God promised to drive out the nations before them, and He cautioned His people not to follow the abominations of those people.

*"When you come into the land which the Lord your God is giving you, you shall not learn to follow the **abominations** of those nations. There shall not be found among you anyone who makes his son or his daughter pass through the fire, or one who practices witchcraft, or a soothsayer, or one who interprets omens, or a sorcerer, or one who calls up the dead. For all who do all these things are an abomination to the LORD, and because of these abominations the LORD your God drives them out before you"* (Deuteronomy 18:9-12).

Jehovah warned His people not to follow after the practices of the nations they were displacing. He was quite clear that their abominations were what had condemned those nations. They were what led to their being driven out of their lands. Note however, that God's remarks concerning these nations and their abominations were made only as it related to His purposes for Israel. Moving through the remainder of the Old Testament, it is apparent that God's primary focus and concern was with the behavior of His covenant people. This is not to say that God was not concerned with the other nations, but Israel was His "special treasure," and they were bound to Him as a wife to her husband. In that sense, Israel's wickedness was much more egregious than that of "the nations."

God was so serious about the possibility of Israel being infected with and affected by the abominations of the heathen nations that He gave them specific instructions to "utterly destroy them." In Deuteronomy 20:16-18, He made it known that to do according to these abominations was to *"sin against the LORD your God"*:

> *"But of the cities of these people which the LORD your God gives you as an inheritance, you shall let nothing that breathes remain alive, but you shall utterly destroy them: the Hittite and the Amorite and the Canaanite and the*

*Perizzite and the Hivite and the Jebusite, just as the LORD your God has commanded you, lest they teach you to do according to all their **abominations** which they have done for their gods, and you sin against the LORD your God."*

The great love that God had for His wife is quite obvious from these texts. It was an exclusive love. He was willing to kill the firstborn of Egypt and then destroy their entire army in order to redeem them and free Israel from her bondage (*"For I am the LORD your God, the Holy One of Israel, your Savior; I gave Egypt for your ransom, Ethiopia and Seba in your place. Since you were precious in My sight, you have been honored, and I have loved you; therefore I will give men for you, and people for your life"* Isaiah 43:3-4).

In Deuteronomy 20, God commanded Israel to "utterly destroy" these nations in order to keep them from going after the false gods of the lands that God was about to give them. Note the way that God repeatedly spoke to these people. He continually identified Himself as *"the LORD your God."* No other people were ever placed in a position of such great privilege and favor. No other people could call upon Jehovah as their God. Even before He had brought them out of Egypt, God made this declaration to Moses: *"I will take you as My people, and I will be your God. Then you shall know that I am the LORD your God who brings you out from under the burdens of the Egyptians"* (Exodus 6:7). He would be Israel's God, as opposed to Egypt's God, in the sense that He was in covenant relationship with Israel alone and He made Himself known to them through their deliverance from the Egyptians.

As noted above, Moses prophesied that Israel would provoke God to jealousy with foreign gods, and yet God revealed Himself to Moses as: *"The LORD, the LORD God, merciful and gracious, longsuffering, and abounding in goodness and truth, keeping mercy for thousands, forgiving iniquity and transgression and sin"* (Exodus 34:6-7). Israel's history of disobedience is recorded throughout the pages of the Old Testament, but also described is the amazing longsuffering of the LORD their God. There would come a time, however, when there would be no place for patience towards His rebellious Old Covenant people. That would be the time when, "the power of the holy (set apart) people has been completely shattered" (Daniel 12:7).

The book of Joshua documented the occupation of the Promised Land by the children of Israel. Even as they saw God drive the people out before them, the book of Judges showed that Israel had not obeyed God's voice. They had not driven all the inhabitants from the land. God promised that these people would *"be thorns in your side, and their gods shall be a snare"* (Judges 2:3). Later in chapter 2, Joshua's passing was described. The Scriptures said:

"They buried him within the border of his inheritance at Timnah Heres, in the mountains of Ephraim, on the north side of Mount Gaash. When all that generation had been gathered to their fathers, another generation arose after them who did not know the LORD nor the work which He had done for Israel. Then the children of Israel did evil in the sight of the LORD, and served the Baals; and they forsook the LORD God of their fathers, who had brought them out of the land of Egypt; and they followed other gods among the gods of the people who were all around them, and they bowed down to them; and the provoked the LORD to anger. They forsook the LORD and served Baal and the Ashtoreths. And the anger of the LORD was hot against Israel. So He delivered them into the hands of their enemies all around, so that they could no longer stand before their enemies. Wherever they went out, the hand of the LORD was against them for calamity, as the LORD had said, and as the LORD had sworn to them. And they were greatly distressed. Nevertheless, the LORD raised up judges who delivered them out of the hand of those who plundered them. Yet they would not listen to their judges, but they

played the harlot with other gods, and bowed down to them. They turned quickly from the way in which their fathers walked, in obeying the commandments of the LORD; they did not do so" (Judges 2:9-17).

This behavior would repeat itself generation after generation. Even one as faithful as Gideon succumbed to the temptation to turn to idolatry. After leading the children of Israel against the Midianites, Gideon took the plunder and, *"made it into an ephod and set it in his city, Ophrah. And all Israel played the harlot with it there. It became a snare to Gideon and to his house"* (Judges 2:27). After his death, it was said, *"that the children of Israel again played the harlot with the Baals, and made Baal-Berith their god. Thus the children of Israel did not remember the LORD their God, who had delivered them from the hands of their enemies on every side"* (Judges 8:33-34).

In the opening chapters of 1 Chronicles, the genealogies of the families of Israel are traced all the way back to Adam. The last segment of chapter 5 addressed the half of the family of Joseph's son Manasseh, who had remained in the land east of the Jordan River. After listing the various leaders, the writer informed the reader that once again these mighty men of valor, famous men, and heads of their father's houses, *"were unfaithful to the God of their fathers, and played the harlot after the gods of the people of the land, whom God had*

61

destroyed before them. So the God of Israel stirred up the spirit of Pul king of Assyria, that is, Tiglath-Pileser king of Assyria. He carried the Reubenites, the Gaddites, and the half-tribe of Manasseh into captivity" (5:25-26).

Chapter 9 of 1 Chronicles begins by concluding that *"all Israel was recorded by genealogies, and indeed, they were inscribed in the book of the kings of Israel. But Judah was carried away captive to Babylon because of their unfaithfulness"* (9:1).

In the days when Solomon's son Rehoboam reigned as king, *"Judah did evil in the sight of LORD, and they provoked Him to jealousy with their sins which they committed, more than all that their fathers had done. For they built for themselves high places, sacred pillars, and wooden images on every high hill and under every green tree. And there were also perverted persons in the land. They did according to all the **abominations** of the nations which the LORD had cast out before the children of Israel"* (1 Kings 14:22-24).

Here again is the language characteristic of intimate relationship. God had been provoked to jealousy by the evil committed by those whom He had so graciously loved, guided, and supplied with abundant provision. Certainly there were other nations whose behavior was equally depraved, and yet nowhere do we find any evidence of God grieving over their unfaithfulness.

In the days when Jehoram was king of
Judah,

> "He made high places in the mountains of
> Judah, and caused the inhabitants of Jerusalem
> to commit harlotry, and led Judah astray. And a
> letter came to him from Elijah the prophet,
> saying, thus says the LORD God of your father
> David: because you have not walked in the ways
> of Jehoshaphat your father, or in the ways of
> Asa king of Judah, but have walked in the way of
> the kings of Israel, and have made Judah and
> the inhabitants of Jerusalem to play the harlot
> like the harlotry of the house of Ahab, and have
> also killed your brothers, those of your father's
> household, who were better than yourself,
> behold, the LORD will strike your people with a
> serious affliction – your children, your wives,
> and all your possessions; and you will become
> very sick with a disease of your intestines, until
> your intestines come out by reason of the
> sickness, day by day" (2 Chronicles 21:11-15).

When Ahaz became Judah's king, it was
said:

*"He did not do what was right in the sight of the LORD, as his father David had done. For he walked in the ways of the kings of Israel, and made molded images for the Baals. He burned incense in the Valley of the Son of Hinnom, and burned children in the fire, according to the **abominations** of nations whom the LORD had cast out before the children of Israel. And he sacrificed and burned incense on the high places, on the hills, and under every green tree. . . the LORD brought Judah low because of Ahaz king of Israel, for he had encouraged moral decline in Judah and had been continually unfaithful to the Lord"* (2 Chronicles 28:1-4, 19).

There are many other passages that could be sited to help establish the nature of the language used by the Old Testament writers in describing Israel's (inclusive of both Israel and Judah after the kingdom split) unfaithfulness to her covenant God. As clear as the language may be in these historical accounts it pales in comparison to the graphic language employed by God's prophets as they were sent to call God's people to repentance.

It is certainly appropriate to look at the language of the Old Testament prophets when studying New Testament prophecy, especially the book of Revelation since it is steeped with Old Testament imagery.

The whole context of Hosea's prophecy is in relation to Israel's harlotry as is laid out in the second verse of chapter 1: *"When the LORD began to speak by Hosea, the LORD said to Hosea: "Go, take yourself a wife of harlotry and children of harlotry, for the land has committed great harlotry by departing from the LORD."* Note how explicitly God links the concept of harlotry with "departing from the LORD." Later in the first verse of chapter 3, God equated Israel's harlotry with adultery: *"Then the LORD said to me, "Go again, love a woman who is loved by a lover and is committing adultery, just like the love of the LORD for the children of Israel, who look to other gods and love the raisin cakes of the pagans."* This imagery is used repeatedly by the "major" prophets.

One of the most graphic and instructive passages is found at the very beginning of Isaiah's vision. It is clear from the beginning that his focus will be primarily on Judah and Jerusalem. His prophecy begins:

> *"The vision of Isaiah the son of Amoz, which he saw concerning Judah and Jerusalem in the days of Uzziah, Jotham, Ahaz, and Hezekiah, kings of Judah. Hear, O heavens, and give ear, O earth! For the LORD has spoken: 'I have*

nourished and brought up children, and they have rebelled against Me; the ox knows its owner and the donkey its master's crib; but Israel does not know, My people do not consider.' Alas, sinful nation, a people laden with iniquity, a brood of evildoers, children who are corrupters! They have forsaken the LORD, they have provoked to anger the Holy One of Israel, they have turned away backward. Why should you be stricken again? You will revolt more and more. The whole head is sick, and the whole heart faints. From the sole of the foot even to the head, there is no soundness in it, but wounds and bruises and putrefying sores; they have not been closed or bound up, or soothed with ointment. . . . How the faithful city has become a **harlot***!* (How critical is this statement when seeking to identify Babylon of Revelation?) *It was full of justice; righteousness lodged in it, but now murderers. Your silver has become dross, your wine mixed with water. Your princes are rebellious, and companions of thieves; everyone loves bribes, and follows after rewards. They do not defend the fatherless, nor does the cause of the widow come before them. Therefore the Lord says, the LORD of hosts, the Mighty One of Israel, 'Ah, I will rid Myself of*

Today!

66

My adversaries, and take vengeance on My enemies'" (Isaiah 1:1-6, 21-24).

This last statement is an obvious reference back to Deuteronomy 32:41-43, where God told Israel what would become of her in her last days. These were the coming days when Israel would provoke her God to jealousy with foreign gods and with abominations, provoke Him to anger (Deuteronomy 32:16).

We should also recall that God told Moses that when he died: *"This people will rise and play the harlot with the gods of the foreigners of the land, where they go to be among them, and they will forsake Me and break My covenant which I have made with them"* (Deuteronomy 31:16). Note well the language used by God when He described Judah as children that He had "nourished and brought up." This is another concept pointing to a unique, special relationship of endearment between God and His people. When God sent Moses from Midian to Egypt to free Israel from their slavery, the Lord told Moses to say to Pharaoh: *"Thus says the LORD: 'Israel is My son, My firstborn. So I say to you, let My son go that he may serve Me. But if you refuse to let him go, indeed I will kill your son, your firstborn'"* (Exodus 4:22-23). As God's firstborn, Israel would be redeemed through the death of Egypt's firstborn sons (Exodus 12). Here God used two terms denoting privileged position in His eyes. Israel was God's son, and as His firstborn, was preeminent over all other nations.

Jeremiah's prophecy was also directed primarily at Judah and Jerusalem. Israel had been carried off by the Assyrians more than a century earlier. Jeremiah pointed back to God's judgment of the Northern tribes with the hope that Judah and Jerusalem would learn from Israel's mistakes. He hoped that they would turn away from their rebellion before God brought similar judgment upon them. God spoke these words to Jeremiah:

> *"Go and cry in the hearing of Jerusalem, saying, 'Thus says the LORD: 'I remember you, the kindness of your youth, the love of your betrothal, when you went after Me in the wilderness, in a land not sown. Israel was holiness to the LORD, the firstfruits of His increase. All that devour him will offend; disaster will come upon them,' says the LORD.' Hear the word of the LORD, O house of Jacob and all the families of the house of Israel. Thus says the LORD: 'What injustice have your fathers found in Me, that they have gone far from Me, have followed idols, and have become idolaters? . . . I brought you into a bountiful country, to eat its fruit and its goodness. But*

when you entered, you defiled My land and made My heritage an abomination" (Jeremiah 2:1-5, 7).

God reflected upon His love as it was manifested toward Israel after having brought her out of Egypt. He had entered into a covenant (betrothal - marriage) relationship with these people so precious to Him. He promised that disaster would come upon the one who tried to devour His people. However, despite all that He had done for them, they had become idolaters and had turned His heritage (Israel – see Jeremiah 12:7, Joel 3:2, Micah 7:14) into an abomination. He said much the same thing in Jeremiah 2:20: *"For of old I have broken your yoke and burst your bonds; and you said, 'I will not transgress,' when on every high hill and under every green tree you lay down, playing the harlot."*

Moving on to the next chapter, there is additional evidence of God's great love and longsuffering towards Judah. God said to them, *"But you have played the harlot with many lovers; yet return to Me"* (Jeremiah 3:1). Despite their unfaithfulness, God was willing to take them back. The Lord said, *"you have polluted the land with your harlotries and your wickedness"* (v.2). Because of this God had withheld the showers and there had been no latter rain. He continued speaking to Jeremiah, reminding him of how He dealt with Israel.

*"The LORD said also to me in the days of Josiah the king: 'Have you seen what backsliding Israel has done? She has gone up on every high mountain and under every green tree, and there played the **harlot**. And I said, after she had done all these things, 'Return to Me.' But she did not return. And her treacherous sister Judah saw it. Then I saw that for all the causes for which backsliding Israel had committed **adultery**, I had put her away and given her a certificate of divorce; yet her treacherous sister Judah did not fear, but went and played the **harlot** also. So it came to pass, through her casual **harlotry**, that she defiled the land and committed **adultery** with stones and trees"* (Jeremiah 3:6-9).

This passage is filled with terms related to marriage. Israel had already been divorced because of her adultery - she had played the harlot. Yet her sister Judah had not feared, but went and played the harlot as well. Clearly both Israel and Judah had been in a marriage relationship with Jehovah, even as the kingdom had been divided.

Note that the concepts of harlotry and adultery are essentially interchangeable in this passage and Israel's harlotry was the grounds for God's complaint against her. Harlotry is seen expressly in the context of the covenant relationship between God and Israel. God pleaded with both houses and they would not heed His call to return. He had sent Israel into captivity, in essence divorcing her (this is precisely the language God used). Even so, we find evidence in Hosea that He would remarry those who would turn to Him. Having been dispersed among the Gentiles, they had reached a state of being in which they were no longer a people in the eyes of God (Hosea 1:9). His amazing love, however, would not allow them to be forgotten and completely rejected. He told them that there would come a day when they would again be "a people" in His eyes (Hosea 1:10; 2:23, 1 Peter 2:10, Romans 9:25-26).

Moving on through Jeremiah's prophecy, God continued to plead with these disobedient people. He said: *"I have seen your adulteries and your lustful neighings, the lewdness of your harlotry, your abominations on the hills in the fields. Woe to you, O Jerusalem! Will you still not be made clean?"* (Jeremiah 13:27). (Note that adultery, harlotry and abominations are used synonymously.) A time came, however, when God's patience was exhausted.

> *"The incense that you burned in the cities of Judah and in the streets of Jerusalem, you and your fathers, your kings and your princes, and the people of the land, did not the LORD remember them, and did it not come into His mind? So the LORD could*

71

*no longer bear it, because of the evil of your doings and because of the **abominations** which you committed. Therefore your land is a desolation, an astonishment, a curse, and without an inhabitant, as it is this day. Because you have burned incense and because you have sinned against the LORD, and have not obeyed the voice of the LORD or walked in His law, in His statutes or in His testimonies, therefore this calamity has happened to you, as at this day"* (Jeremiah 44:21-23).

Because of their unfaithfulness, God had finally brought the Babylonians against them to destroy their city and temple and to take the people away into captivity.

The images that permeate the prophecy of Ezekiel are incredibly powerful in their condemnation of Israel and Jerusalem. In chapter two, God said: *"Son of man, I am sending you to the children of Israel, to a rebellious nation that has rebelled against Me"* (2:3). This concept of Israel as a rebellious people is repeated numerous times in this prophecy. In chapter five, He said: *"Because of all your **abominations** . . . you who remain I will scatter to all the winds"* (Ezekiel 5:9-10). Among other things, He said: *"Pestilence and blood shall pass through you, and I will bring the sword against you. I, the LORD, have spoken"* (Ezekiel 5:17).

72

There is so much anger in these words, and yet we must see that it is all as a result of Israel turning away from her Husband. God mingled mercy with His promise of judgment against the unfaithful people.

> *"'Yet I will leave a remnant, so that you may have some who escape the sword among the nations, when you are scattered through the countries. Then those of you who escape will remember Me among the nations where they are carried captive, because I was crushed by their **adulterous** heart which has departed from Me, and by their eyes which play the **harlot** after their idols; they will loathe themselves for the evils which they committed in all their **abominations**. And they shall know that I am the Lord; I have not said in vain that I would bring calamity upon them.' 'Thus says the LORD GOD: 'Pound your fists and stamp your feet, and say, 'Alas, for all the evil **abominations** of the house of Israel! For they shall fall by the sword, by famine, and by pestilence"* (Ezekiel 6:8-11: compare this last statement with Revelation 6).

Notice the anguish in God's words as He spoke of being, *"crushed by their adulterous heart which has departed from*

Me." Surely these are the haunting words of the Husband of an unfaithful wife. As is the case throughout much of Ezekiel, God charged Israel with committing evil abominations. They are at the heart of the venom of His words. This is seen again in chapter seven, where once again God cried to Israel through His prophet:

> *"And you, son of man, thus says the LORD GOD to the land of Israel: 'An end! The end has come upon the four corners of the land. Now the end has come upon you, and I will send My anger against you; I will judge you according to your ways, and I will repay you for your* **abominations**. *My eye will not spare you, nor will I have pity; but I will repay your ways, and your* **abominations** *will be in your midst; then you shall know that I am the LORD!'"* (Ezekiel 7:2-4).

In chapter 8, God showed Ezekiel the abominations being committed in the temple; the abominations that were driving Him away from His sanctuary. *"Son of man, do you see what they are doing, the great* **abominations** *that the house of Israel commits here, to make Me go far away from My sanctuary?"* (Ezekiel 8:6). After showing him all these abominations, God said: *"Have you seen all this, O son of man? Is it a trivial thing to the house of Israel to commit the* **abominations** *which they* *commit here? For they have filled the land with violence; then they have returned to provoke Me to anger. Indeed they put the branch to their nose. Therefore I also will act in fury. My eyes will not spare nor will I have pity; and though they cry in My ears with a loud voice, I will not hear them"* (Ezekiel 8:17-18). What Ezekiel saw next was astounding. He saw the glory depart from the temple in chapter 10, followed by a portrayal of Judah's captivity. In chapter 12, God warned that judgment would not be postponed. Next, God's condemnation fell upon Israel's foolish prophets, who had cried out *"Peace! when there is no peace"* (Ezekiel 13:10).

When the idolatrous elders approached Ezekiel and sat before him, God responded by saying,

> *"Should I let Myself be inquired of at all by them? Therefore speak to them, and say to them, 'Thus says the LORD GOD: 'Everyone of the house of Israel who <u>sets his idols in his heart,</u> and puts before him what causes him to stumble into iniquity, and then comes to the prophet, I the LORD will answer him who comes, according to the multitude of his idols, that I may seize the house of Israel by their heart, because they are all estranged from Me by their idols.'' 'Therefore say to the house of Israel, 'Thus says the LORD GOD: 'Repent, turn away*

from your idols, and turn your faces away from
*all your **abominations**. For anyone of the house*
of Israel, or of the strangers who dwell in Israel,
who separates himself from Me and <u>sets up idols</u>
<u>in his heart</u> and puts before him what causes
him to stumble into iniquity, then comes to a
prophet to inquire of him concerning Me, I the
LORD will answer him by Myself. I will set My
face against that man and make him a sign and
a proverb, and I will cut him off from the midst
of My people. Then you shall know that I am the
LORD" (Ezekiel 14:3-8).

Even in the midst of this powerful condemnation and warning, we find God still reaching out to His people. He was grieved that these people had set up idols in their hearts, in place of the Lord. This was the Lord who had, time after time throughout Israel's history, identified Himself to Israel as *"the LORD your God."* We can feel the anguish of His heart as He expressed the desire to *"seize the house of Israel by their heart."* He called them to *"Repent, turn away from your idols, and turn your faces away from all your **abominations**."* How longsuffering was God towards His unfaithful wife and how great the love that drove Him to plead with them through His prophet!

Nevertheless, judgment was coming and in chapter 15 God turned to the imagery of Jerusalem as a vine; a vine that was to be destroyed by fire. *"Like the wood of the vine among the trees of the forest, which I have given to the fire for fuel, so I will give up the inhabitants of Jerusalem; and I will set My face against them. They will go out from one fire, but another fire shall devour them. Then you shall know that I am the Lord, when I set My face against them. Thus I will make the land desolate, because they have persisted in unfaithfulness,'* says *the LORD GOD"* (Ezekiel 15:4-8). At every turn, all throughout their history, Israel's problems had been caused by her persistent unfaithfulness toward the One who had created and loved her, and had redeemed her from Egypt.

On and on we could go in this incredible prophecy. Indeed it is essential that the student of God's word do precisely that so that the language and the images that pervade these visions become ingrained in the mind.

The picture of the harlot sisters painted for us in Ezekiel 23 must bear heavily upon us when looking at Revelation 16 and 17. The whole of chapter 23 presents as clear a case as could be desired to definitively show that the concepts of harlotry and adultery are essentially synonymous and inextricably linked to the abominations committed by Jerusalem. All are united in their reflection of Jerusalem's covenant disobedience. These concepts are contextually interchangeable as the prophet spoke of Jerusalem chasing after her lovers and worshipping idols made with hands. Although it may be more common in our day

77

to think of harlotry as synonymous with prostitution, the Old Testament clearly associates harlotry, in its primary sense, almost exclusively within the context of *marital unfaithfulness to Yahweh.* This is tremendously important.

If the contention that Babylon of Revelation represents Old Covenant Jerusalem/Judah (as a people) is indeed true, it is legitimate to ponder why God would have used this city to represent His covenant people. If the history of the southern tribes is recalled, it is apparent that there is a unique and intimate connection between the southern kingdom and Babylon.

Assyria had previously scattered the northern tribes throughout their empire, but God had spared Judah from this assault. Years later, however, it was the Babylonians who had come and destroyed the city of Jerusalem and taken much of the population into captivity – many of them removed to Babylon. Much has been written regarding the influence of the Babylonian culture as it pertains to Jews taken into captivity. A large portion of the Jews who were deported to Babylon chose to stay there when offered the opportunity to return to Jerusalem to help rebuild the city and the temple. Many of the basic concepts of the Babylonian religion and culture influenced the thought and culture of those Jews remaining in Babylon. The influence of Babylon in turning many Jews away from their heritage under the Mosaic covenant was unlike that of any other people in ancient Jewish history.

The book of Daniel demonstrates that there was a relatively small number of Jews who remained faithful to their God. For the most part, Babylon was a wicked and debauched kingdom and many of the Jews had been assimilated into that culture. Daniel described in chapter five how King Belshazzar took the vessels that Nebuchadnezzar had taken from the temple in Jerusalem and used them in drunken revelry in praise of the gods of gold and silver, bronze, iron, wood, and stone (v.4). Here were a people steeped in wickedness using these sacred vessels as instruments of their idolatry. It is not hard to draw a parallel between this kingdom so closely associated with the Jews and the scathing words of Jesus spoken to the hypocritical scribes and Pharisees: *"Woe to you, scribes and Pharisees, hypocrites! For you cleanse the outside of the cup and dish, but inside they are full of extortion and self-indulgence"* (Matthew 23:25). See also the somewhat parallel passage of Luke 11:39 where Jesus said that their inward part is full of greed and wickedness.

Early in chapter 23 of Ezekiel's prophecy we find a description of Jerusalem's illicit relationship with Babylon with whom she entered "into the bed of love." Oholibah (Jerusalem) had lusted for and committed adultery with the Chaldeans (Babylon). Because of her harlotry (synonymous with adultery) committed with Babylon, God said that He had alienated Himself from Jerusalem just as He had with her sister (Oholah – Israel).

> *"Now although her sister Oholibah saw this, she became more corrupt in her lust than she, and in her harlotry more corrupt than her sister's harlotry. "She lusted for the neighboring Assyrians, captains and rulers, clothed most gorgeously, horsemen riding on horses, all of them desirable young men. Then I saw that she was defiled; both took the same way. But she increased her harlotry; she looked at men portrayed on the wall, images of Chaldeans portrayed in vermilion, girded with belts around their waists, flowing turbans on their heads, all of them looking like captains, in the manner of the Babylonians of Chaldea, the land of their nativity. As soon as her eyes saw them, she lusted for them and sent messengers to them in Chaldea. "Then the Babylonians came to her, into the bed of love, and they defiled her with their immorality; so she was defiled by them, and alienated herself from them. She revealed her harlotry and uncovered her nakedness. Then I alienated Myself from her, as I had alienated Myself from her sister"* (Ezekiel 23:11-18 – note

the possible implications for our understanding of Ephesians 2:12 and Colossians 1:21).

As is seen in the last verses of Daniel 5, Babylon had been weighed in the balances and found wanting (v. 27). That very night the kingdom was taken away from her. The end of the Babylonian kingdom may well be seen as foreshadowing the end of Israel's Old Covenant "kingdom."

It should be very obvious that God's displeasure (as expressed through the words of His Son) towards the religious leaders of Old Covenant Jerusalem was much like God's rejection of the Babylonian kingdom. Jesus did indeed promise these religious leaders (those He had identified as an adulterous generation in Matthew 12:39, 16:4, and Mark 8:38) that, *"the kingdom of God will be taken from you and given to a nation bearing the fruits of it"* (Matthew 21:43). So the parallel is clearly there and from a biblical perspective, who would more readily exemplify Jerusalem of Jesus' generation than ancient Babylon?   Jerusalem = Babylon

Ezekiel chapter 24 finds God again referring to Jerusalem as "the bloody city" (vv.6 and 9). Nowhere else in the scriptures do we find any other city, or people, described and characterized with such specific and graphic language that so precisely reflects the titles ascribed to the great city of Revelation. This is the very city to whom Jesus said: *"That*

upon you may come all the righteous blood shed on the earth"
(Matthew 23:35).

Ezekiel 16 and the Harlot

Perhaps the *coup de grace*, what should be the death knell to all speculation of Babylon being anyone other than Old Covenant Jerusalem and all that she represented, is found in the 16th chapter of Ezekiel.

God began the chapter in much the same manner as is often seen throughout this prophesy. *"Son of man, cause Jerusalem to know her **abominations"** (v.2). Instead, however, of proceeding to condemn her, He reviewed and recounted the establishment of His covenant relationship with Israel. He spoke of her birth and nativity as she struggled as it were as an infant, when *"you were thrown out into the open field, when you yourself were loathed on the day you were born"* (v.5). He then described with poetic imagery how He came to her rescue and showered her with unspeakable love.

> *"And when I passed by you and saw you struggling in your own blood, I said to you in your blood, 'Live!' Yes, I said to you in your blood, 'Live!' I made you thrive like a plant in the field; and you grew, matured, and became very beautiful. Your breasts were formed, your hair grew, but you were naked and bare. When I passed by you again and looked upon you, indeed your time was the time of love; so I spread My wings over you and covered your*

nakedness. Yes, I swore an oath to you and entered into a covenant with you, and you became mine," says the LORD GOD. "Then I washed you in water; yes I thoroughly washed off your blood, and I anointed you with oil. I clothed you in embroidered cloth and gave you sandals of badger skin; I clothed you with fine linen and covered you with silk. I adorned you with ornaments, put bracelets on your wrists, and a chain on your neck. And put a jewel in your nose, earrings in your ears, and a beautiful crown on your head. Thus you were adorned with gold and silver, and your clothing was of fine linen, silk, and embroidered cloth. You ate pastry of fine flour, honey, and oil. You were exceedingly beautiful, and succeeded to royalty. Your fame went out among the nations because of your beauty, for it was perfect through My splendor which I had bestowed on you,' says the LORD GOD" (Ezekiel 16:6-14).

God's cry to "Live!" was a call to covenant relationship and hearkens back to Deuteronomy 30:15, 19, etc.. To "live" in this biblical sense was to be in covenant relationship with God. (The promise of resurrection was the promise of renewal of covenant relationship through the New Covenant).

Covenant imagery abounds as God said He would spread His wings over her and cover her nakedness. This is imagery found in various places throughout the scriptures. God brought Israel into a marriage relationship in which their intimacy was to be exclusive. Her nakedness would be covered by her husband and was no longer to be seen by others. For her nakedness to be uncovered was indication of unfaithfulness or a break in this covenant relationship. What a glorious picture of God's boundless love, as He lavished upon Israel the finest of every provision. He spoke of her as a proud husband would speak of his cherished and beloved wife. He spoke of her exceeding beauty, the perfection of her beauty as God had bestowed His splendor upon her.

One can hardly imagine a more resplendent description of overwhelming love being showered by any man upon his true love. Alas, it all appeared to be for naught. In the very next verse, God began to describe, in great detail, Jerusalem's harlotry.

> *"But you trusted in your own beauty, played the **harlot** because of your fame, and poured out your **harlotry** on everyone passing by who would have it. You took some of your garments and adorned multicolored high places for yourself, and played the **harlot** on them. Such things should not happen, nor be. You have also*

*taken your beautiful jewelry from My gold and silver, which I had given you, and made yourself male images and played the **harlot** with them. You took your embroidered garments and covered them, and you set My oil and My incense before them. Also My food which I gave you – the pastry of fine flour, oil, and honey which I fed you – you set it before them as sweet incense; and so it was,' says the Lord GOD. 'Moreover you took your sons and your daughters, whom you bore to Me, and these you sacrificed to them to be devoured. Were your acts of **harlotry** a small matter, that you have slain My children and offered them up to them by causing them to pass through the fire? And in all your **abominations** and acts of **harlotry** you did not remember the days of your youth, when you were naked and bare, struggling in your blood.' . . . 'How degenerate is your heart!' says the Lord GOD, 'seeing you do all these things, the deeds of a brazen **harlot**'"* (Ezekiel 16:15-22, 30).

Jerusalem had taken all that the Lord had given her and flaunted it before Him. They had made idols and played the harlot with them. It was as if they could no longer see that it was God who had given all these things to her out of His great love. Jehovah had warned Israel, as they prepared to enter the Promised Land, not to forget from whence came all of her benefits.

"Therefore you shall keep the commandments of the LORD your God, to walk in His ways and to fear Him. For the LORD your God is bringing you into a good land, a land of brooks of water, of fountains and springs, that flow out of valleys and hills; a land of wheat and barley, of vines and fig trees and pomegranates, a land of olive oil and honey; a land in which you will eat bread without scarcity, in which you will lack nothing; a land whose stones are iron and out of whose hills you can dig copper. When you have eaten and are full, then you shall bless the LORD your God for the good land which He has given you. "Beware that you do not forget the LORD your God by not keeping His commandments, His judgments, and His statutes which I command you today, lest—when you have eaten and are full, and have built beautiful houses and dwell in them; and when your herds and your flocks multiply, and your silver and your gold are multiplied, and all that you have is multiplied; when your heart is lifted up, and you forget the LORD your God who brought you out

87

of the land of Egypt, from the house of bondage;
who led you through that great and terrible
wilderness, in which were fiery serpents and
scorpions and thirsty land where there was no
water; who brought water for you out of the
flinty rock; who fed you in the wilderness with
manna, which your fathers did not know, that He
might humble you and that He might test you, to
do you good in the end— then you say in your
heart, 'My power and the might of my hand have
gained me this wealth'" (Deuteronomy 8:6-17).

Here are many of the same blessings described in Ezekiel, only with differing imagery. Jerusalem had trusted in her own beauty – in other words, she had forgotten what God had done for her in the days of her youth, and had in essence said: *"My power and the might of my hand have gained me this wealth."*

The previous section of Ezekiel 16 focuses on the image of the marriage relationship, with God speaking to Jerusalem of the children that she bore Him. All of the things cited by God in Ezekiel 16:16-19 were simply Israel's blatant rejection of her great benefactor; almost as if she were despising Him and spitting in His face. In verse 32, God said that she was *"an adulterous wife, who takes strangers instead of her husband."* In verse 30, God had likened her

88

to a *"brazen harlot."* She even went beyond the typical practice of a harlot. Rather than receiving payment for her harlotry, she made payment to her lovers.

> *"You erected your shrine at the head of every road, and built your high place in every street. Yet you were not like a harlot, because you scorned payment. You are an **adulterous wife**, who takes strangers instead of her husband. Men make payment to all harlots, but you made your payments to all your lovers, and hired them to come to you from all around for your **harlotry**. You are the opposite of other women in your **harlotry**, because no one solicited you to be a **harlot**. In that you gave payment but no payment was given you, therefore you are the opposite"* (Ezekiel 16:31-34).

It requires no stretch of the imagination to see that she could, and indeed should from a biblical perspective, be called the "mother of harlots"! The use of this terminology attests to the extended history of infidelity which could really only apply to God's unfaithful Old Covenant people. It also clearly shows that Israel's harlotry was the basis for her being termed an *adulterous* wife.

Beginning in verse 35, God spoke very forcefully to Jerusalem, with words promising judgment because she had been unfaithful to her Husband. In verse 36, God spoke of Israel's unfaithfulness in uncovering her nakedness through her harlotry, and then in verse 37 it is said that it is God who would uncover her nakedness to her lovers. This would seem to be a promise of divorce, of being cast away – no longer in covenant relationship.

*"Now then, O **harlot**, hear the word of the LORD! Thus says the Lord GOD: 'Because your filthiness was poured out and your nakedness uncovered in your **harlotry** with your lovers, and with all your abominable idols, and because of the blood of your children which you gave to them, surely, therefore, I will gather all your lovers with whom you took pleasure, all those you loved, and all those you hated; I will gather them from all around against you and will uncover your nakedness to them, that they may see all your nakedness. And I will judge you as women who break wedlock or shed blood are judged; I will bring blood upon you in fury and jealousy. I will also give you into their hand, and they shall throw down your shrines and break down your high places. They shall also strip you of your clothes, take your beautiful*

*jewelry, and leave you naked and bare. They shall also bring up an assembly against you, and they shall stone you with stones and thrust you through with their swords. They shall burn your houses with fire, and execute judgments on you in the sight of many women; and I will make you cease playing the harlot, and you shall no longer hire lovers. So I will lay to rest My fury toward you, and My jealousy shall depart from you. I will be quiet, and angry no more. Because you did not remember the days of your youth, but agitated Me with all these things, surely I will also recompense your deeds on your own head,' says the Lord GOD. 'And you shall not commit lewdness in addition to all your **abominations***"* (Ezekiel 16:35-43).

Once again God spoke of His jealousy, but what is so striking in this extended passage is that we find so many important parallels with the prophecy against Babylon in Revelation chapters 17 and 18. In Revelation 17:3-4, John, *"saw a woman sitting on a scarlet beast which was full of names of blasphemy, having seven heads and ten horns. The woman was arrayed in purple and scarlet, and adorned with gold and precious stones* (see Ezekiel 16:10-13) *and pearls, having in her hand a golden cup full of abominations and the filthiness of her fornication."*

Revelation 17:7 said that the beast with the seven heads and ten horns carried the woman (Babylon the great in Revelation 17:5). The ten horns are identified in Revelation 17:12 as ten kings and correspond to her lovers, because Revelation 18:3 says that *"the kings of the earth* (The Greek word **Ge** can be translated as land or "a country, land enclosed within fixed boundaries, a tract of land, territory, region" and certainly does not necessarily imply the whole earth) *have committed fornication with her."*

Just as God said that He would gather Jerusalem's lovers against her, so we find that, *"the ten horns which you saw on the beast, these will hate the harlot, make her desolate and naked, eat her flesh and burn her with fire"* (Revelation 17:16). In Revelation 18, these words were spoken of Babylon, that mighty city (v.10): *"The fruit that your soul longed for has gone from you, and all the things which are rich and splendid have gone from you, and you shall find them no more at all. . .. For in one hour such great riches came to nothing"* (Revelation 18:14, 17).

In the same way that God said Jerusalem's lovers would do to her (*"I will also give you into their hand, and they shall throw down your shrines and break down your high places. They shall strip you of your clothes, take your beautiful jewelry, and leave you naked and bare. . . They shall burn your houses with fire"* (Ezekiel 16:39,41; see also Ezekiel 23:28-30). So the ten

92

horns (Babylon's lovers) would make Babylon desolate and naked and burn her with fire. This follows precisely the pattern set in Ezekiel 16. As scripture interprets scripture, this points directly to the Babylon of Revelation as representative of Old Covenant Jerusalem.

These and other parallels are all intricately tied to the closely related concepts of adultery, harlotry, fornication and abominations committed in unfaithfulness. For these things, as well as her shedding of innocent blood, God promised to judge Jerusalem, i.e. Babylon of Revelation. No other entity is ever accused of being a harlot or shedding innocent blood. God finished this section of Ezekiel's prophecy with one final litany of Jerusalem's lewdness and her abominations.

In Ezekiel 16:44-57, God spoke of Jerusalem's sister Samaria, who He called Sodom because of her abominations. As bad as these abominations had been, God told Jerusalem that, *"Samaria did not commit half of your sins; but you have multiplied your **abominations** more than they"* (Ezekiel 16:51). The Lord GOD then said: *"I will deal with you as you have done, who despised the oath by breaking the covenant"* (v.59).

In essence God was stating that Jerusalem had despised the covenant and upon her would fall the covenant curses described in Deuteronomy 28-30 and Leviticus 26. In Deuteronomy 28:59-60, Israel was told that because of her disobedience, *"the LORD will bring upon you and your descendants extraordinary plagues - great and prolonged plagues - and serious and prolonged sicknesses. Moreover He will bring back on you all the diseases of Egypt, of which you were afraid, and they shall cling to you"* (see also 32:27).

It would be wise to look more closely at the two chapters noted directly above. God's covenant relationship with Israel is a theme that dominates the Old Testament and that relationship is the context in which the New Testament documents come to us.

Both Leviticus 26 and Deuteronomy 28 clearly proclaim how God intended to deal with Israel and it is all contingent upon Israel's obedience to the terms of the Mosaic Covenant. These two passages are immensely important. Yet, far too few commentators even take note of them in their analysis of the book of Revelation. However, if it is properly understood that the New Testament is focused upon the dissolution of the Mosaic Covenant and the subsequent coming of the promised new and everlasting covenant, then their importance may be more fully appreciated.

In these two chapters, God clearly defined what would become of Israel if she did not, *"perform all My commandments, but break My covenant"* (Leviticus 26:15). It should be quite clear that Israel (both the northern and southern kingdoms) had not kept His commandments.

Without going into exhaustive detail, there are several key passages in these two chapters that should be examined more closely in relation to several passages found in the book of Revelation. If God was to be truly righteous and just in His dealing with Israel then it should be expected that He would meet out upon her that which was due her as a result of her unfaithfulness. It is also reasonable to expect that this judgment would be proclaimed as a manifest demonstration that God's judgments are true and just (see Revelation 16:7 and 19:2). Coming forth from this judgment, as God dispensed with those who had rejected His loving provisions as Husband to Israel, was the promised new covenant (re- marriage) for the faithful remnant (Isaiah 10:20-22, 11:11-16; Jeremiah 23:3, 31:1-8; Joel 2:32; Micah 2:12). Certainly that is what is found being played out in the fall of Babylon the great of Revelation and the subsequent announcement of the marriage of the Lamb.

> *"I will set My face against you, and you shall be defeated by your enemies. Those who hate you shall reign over you, and you shall flee when no one pursues you. 'And after all this, if you do not obey Me, then I will punish you seven times more for your sins. I will break the pride of your power; I will make your heavens like iron and*

your earth like bronze. And your strength shall be spent in vain; for your land shall not yield its produce, nor shall the trees of the land yield their fruit. 'Then, if you walk contrary to Me, and are not willing to obey Me, I will bring on you seven times more plagues, according to your sins. I will also send wild beasts among you, which shall rob you of your children, destroy your livestock, and make you few in number; and your highways shall be desolate. 'And if by these things you are not reformed by Me, but walk contrary to Me, then I also will walk contrary to you, and I will punish you yet seven times for your sin" (Leviticus 26:17-24).

At this point we cannot ignore the powerful picture in Revelation 11:8, of, *"the great city which spiritually is called Sodom and Egypt, where also our Lord was crucified."* Neither can we ignore the striking correlation between the plagues described as the bowls of wrath poured out in Revelation 16, and the plagues that God poured out upon Egypt in Exodus 7-10 (note also the locusts of Revelation 9). Because of her disobedience, God likened Jerusalem (representative of Old Covenant Israel) to Sodom and Egypt. In the end, God would destroy her just as He had done with her spiritual predecessors.

As was the case with Jerusalem in Ezekiel's day, so it was with Babylon in John's vision. In chapter 18 came the cry of, *"another voice from heaven saying, 'Come out of her, my people* (refer to Luke 21:21-22), *lest you receive of her plagues. For her sins have reached to heaven and God has remembered her iniquities. Render to her just as she rendered to you and repay her double according to her works; in the cup which she has mixed, mix double for her. . . . Therefore her plagues will come in one day - death and mourning and famine. And she will be utterly burned with fire, for strong is the Lord God who judges her"* (Revelation 18:4-6,8).

If we allow scripture to interpret scripture, we must turn back to the Old Testament and God's words spoken through his prophet Jeremiah to Israel: *"For My eyes are on all their ways; they are not hidden from My face, nor is their iniquity hidden from My eyes. And first I will repay double for their iniquity and their sin, because they have defiled My land; they have filled My inheritance with the carcasses of their detestable and abominable idols"* (16:17-18; see also Isaiah 40:2 where the same imagery is used).

Nowhere in the Scriptures do we find God speaking to any people other than Israel in this manner. It stands to reason that Revelation 18 must be seen in the context of, and in reference to, His covenant people. The parallels are too precise to dismiss. Revelation 18 said that Babylon's sins, *"have reached* to heaven and God has remembered her iniquities" (v.5), while Jeremiah concludes that God's "eyes are on all their ways; they are not hidden from My face, nor is their iniquity hidden from My eyes" (Jeremiah 16:17). The response is exactly the same: "repay her double according to her works" (Revelation 18:6), and "repay double for their iniquity and their sin" (Jeremiah 16:8). To attribute this passage in Revelation 18 to anyone other than Jerusalem is to move outside the context of scripture.

Imbedded within this passage from Revelation 18 is the statement that "God has remembered her iniquities" (v.5). This phrase reflected the basic nature of the Old Covenant. After discussing the impotence of the Old Covenant sacrifices, the writer of Hebrews had this to say: "But in those sacrifices there is a reminder of sins every year. For it is impossible that the blood of bulls and goats could take away sin" (10:3-4). This was the weakness of the Old Covenant.

As the vision of Revelation comes to its climax, God remembered Jerusalem's iniquities and was preparing to finally pour out the wrath of His covenant curses in response to her covenant unfaithfulness. This was typical of God's response to Israel's sins. When it was said that He remembered her sins, it was invariably stated that He would punish them. In Hosea 8:13 it was said: "For the sacrifices of My offerings they sacrifice flesh and eat it, but the LORD does not accept them.

Now He will remember their iniquity and punish their sins." In 9:9 the prophet spoke of Israel: *"They are deeply corrupted, as in the days of Gibeah. He will remember their iniquity; He will punish their sins."* Similar words came through the prophet Jeremiah. *"Thus says the LORD to this people: 'Thus they have loved to wander; they have not restrained their feet. Therefore the LORD does not accept them; He will remember their iniquity now, and punish their sins'"* (Jeremiah 14:10).

As the vision continued and it was prophetically and proleptically announced that Babylon had fallen, the great multitude in heaven sang the praises of God: *"For true and righteous are His judgments, because He has judged the great harlot who corrupted the earth* (land) *with her fornication"* (Revelation 19:2). In what sense was God true and righteous in His judgment? *He was being true to the terms of the covenant that He had made with Israel.*

The covenant terms were very plain in promising blessings for obedience, but even more clear and explicit in its declaration of definite judgment in the event of disobedience. God had always been incredibly longsuffering toward the weaknesses and failures of His people, but the time had come when the cumulative measure of their sins was finished or filled up. Jesus had told the Jews of His generation, to *"fill up the measure of your fathers guilt"* (Matthew 23:32). He had said that they would persecute and kill His prophets, wise men and scribes. It was for this reason, *"that on you may come all the righteous blood shed on the earth, from the blood of righteous Abel to the blood of Zechariah, son of Berechiah, whom you murdered between the temple and the altar. Assuredly, I say to you, all these things will come upon this generation"* (Matthew 23:35-36).

The people (the Jews) had been warned by Jesus and the warnings continued in the message of His 1st century disciples. God's only true and righteous path was to be faithful to the covenant by pouring out all the covenant curses against those who rejected the One who had come in fulfillment of all the types and shadows of the old Law. As the Christ fulfilled them, what was left of that Old Covenant system, along with those who clung to it and would not embrace the New, would now have to be cast out and destroyed. Jesus had come to fulfill the promise of a New Covenant that would restore Israel's broken relationship with their God.

With the passing of the Old, as God remembered Israel's iniquities and prepared to destroy her, the New was being fully consummated. In contradistinction with the Old Covenant, Jeremiah promised a New Covenant which was not according to the covenant that God made with the fathers. This covenant would address the weakness of that old covenant. God said: *"I will forgive their iniquity, and their sin I will remember no more"* (Jeremiah 31:34). The writer of Hebrews quoted

100

Jeremiah twice (Hebrews 8:2 & 10:17) and after the first he followed with this comment: *"In that He says, 'A new covenant.' He has made the first obsolete. Now what is becoming obsolete and growing old is ready to vanish away"* (Hebrews 8:13).

Many today teach that the old or first covenant passed away at the cross, but here the writer said that while it is obsolete, it had not as yet passed away. This is in fact what was taking place in Revelation. The passing of the old and the consummation of the new are inseparably linked. The cry went forth, *"Rejoice over her, O heaven, and you holy apostles and prophets, for God has avenged you on her!"* (18:20) announcing that Babylon had fallen. This was followed immediately by the call: *"Let us be glad and rejoice and give Him glory, for the marriage of the Lamb has come, and His wife has made herself ready"* (19:7).

Here is the marriage of those who had been betrothed to Christ as a chaste virgin (2 Corinthians 11:2). Christ had sanctified and cleansed her so that He might present her to Himself. This is the bride to whom the Lamb was to be wedded through the promised New Covenant.

The same concept is expressed with different imagery in Revelation 21, which followed immediately upon the scene of the "Great White Throne Judgment" of chapter 20:11-15.

101

"Now I saw a new heaven and a new earth, for the first heaven and the first earth had passed away. Also there was no more sea. Then I, John saw the holy city, New Jerusalem, coming down out of heaven from God, prepared as a bride adorned for her husband" (21:1-2). Clearly this is covenantal imagery - imagery of one covenant passing away (Hebrews 8:13) and the approaching marriage, signifying the consummation of the New Covenant that had been inaugurated with Christ's shed blood.

NC
faithful

Looking back again to Revelation 18, it should bring to mind Jesus' parable of the Wedding Feast in Matthew 22. Verse 8 of Revelation 18, says that Babylon, *"will be utterly burned with fire"* (recall also Ezekiel 16:41). Hear Jesus' words as He spoke to the chief priests and Pharisees:

> *"The kingdom of heaven is like a certain king who arranged a marriage for his son, and sent out his servants to call those who were invited to the wedding; and they were not willing to come. Again, he sent out other servants, saying, 'Tell those who are invited, 'See, I have prepared my dinner; my oxen and fatted cattle are killed, and all things are ready. Come to the wedding.'' But they made light of it and went their ways, one to his own farm, another to his business. And the rest seized his servants, treated them spitefully,*

and killed them. But when the king heard about it, he was furious. And he sent out his armies, destroyed those murderers, and burned up their city. Then he said to his servants, 'The wedding is ready, but those who were invited were not worthy. Therefore go into the highways, and as many as you find, invite to the wedding.' So those servants went out into the highways and gathered together all whom they found, both bad and good. And the wedding hall was filled with guests" (Matthew 22:2-10).

Here it can be seen that all of the things we have discussed are inseparably linked together. As previously discussed, Babylon was to be judged in large part because she was, *"drunk with the blood of the saints and with the blood of the martyrs of Jesus"* (Revelation 17:6). In Jesus' parable it was Israel (they were the ones who the prophets had called to the wedding) who had *"seized his servants, treated them spitefully, and killed them"* (see also Matthew 23:34). It was because of this that, *"The king sent out his armies, destroyed those murderers, and burned their city."* Obviously, *"their city"* was Jerusalem. The correlation is too exact to ignore. The Pharisees knew that Jesus was referring to them and their city when He told this parable, because when they heard it they, *"went out and plotted how they might entangle Him in His talk"* (v.15; also 21:45-

103

46). Just as in Revelation, the destruction of the city is followed immediately by the wedding.

We have now worked our way almost through to the end of Ezekiel 16. We have looked at the promise of judgment against Jerusalem in Jesus' parable of the Wedding Feast in Matthew 22. We have worked our way to the end of Revelation 18 where we are told that, *"with violence the great city Babylon shall be thrown down"* (v.21).

We have now reached a point of climax in all three of these texts. In each the promise of terrible judgment leads directly into a wedding scene, a glorious display of God's mercy and love for His faithful servants. As the judgment of the wicked and disobedient is completed, the Old Covenant, or marriage relationship, had been cast away (see Galatians 4:21-31). Immediately commences the wedding of the Son, the marriage of the Lamb, the establishment of an everlasting covenant (understood as a marriage covenant as had been the case with the Mosaic covenant).

Conclusion

We have looked in some detail at the events surrounding the fall of Babylon and the arrival of the marriage of the Lamb. Let us go back briefly to Ezekiel 16.

In verse 59, God said that He would deal with her as she had done in despising the oath and breaking the covenant: *"And all the people answered with one voice and said, 'All the words which the LORD has said we will do"* (Exodus 24:3; see also verses 7-8 and 19:8). God's mercies never cease, however, and we immediately find Him saying: *"Nevertheless I will remember My covenant with you in the days of your youth, and I will establish an everlasting covenant with you. . . . And I will establish My covenant with you. Then you shall know that I am the LORD, that you may remember and be ashamed, and never open your mouth anymore because of your shame, when I provide you an atonement for all you have done,' says the Lord GOD"* (Ezekiel 16:60, 62-63).

This is tremendously important - the promise of the establishment of this everlasting covenant immediately followed the promise of covenantal judgment and was contextually tied to the provision of atonement for all they had done. As Christ came in judgment at His parousia (presence) in AD 70, he also came as High Priest out of the Holiest of All to consummate the atonement "process" that had been initiated at the cross. This was the final and complete fulfillment of all the types and shadows of the Old Covenant system. This was the glorious appearing of our great God and Savior Jesus Christ (Titus 2:13) that the 1st century Christians had so eagerly awaited (*"To those who eagerly wait for Him He will appear a second time, apart from sin, for salvation"* Hebrews 9:28).

What a remarkable thing to see, if we just stop for a moment to look back at God's words to Israel in Deuteronomy 32. Moses said: *"The LORD will judge His people and have compassion on His servants"* (v. 36). He had said: *"I will render vengeance to My enemies, and repay those who hate Me"* (v. 41). Finally in verse 43, He said: *"Rejoice, O Gentiles, with His people; for He will avenge the blood of His servants, and render vengeance to His adversaries; He will provide atonement for His land and His people."*

All the things that God promised would happen to Israel, we find being fulfilled in John's vision. God's salvation that had been promised so long ago was now fully come. Sin had been dealt a mortal blow. Relationship had been restored, seeing as the marriage of the Lamb had now come and His bride had made herself ready (Revelation 19:7). ***"Alleluia! For the Lord God Omnipotent reigns!"*** (Revelation 19:6)

Suggested Reading:

There is an ever growing body of literature dealing with fulfilled prophecy. This includes many valuable books and pamphlets as well as numerous articles and books available online. Listed below are several websites that contain a wealth of information in addition to a list of suggested books that address a wide range of topics related to the vast scope of fulfilled eschatology, including material discussed in this document. All of the books listed below may be obtained either directly from or through Amazon.com. All of Don Preston's books as well as several others listed below are available through his websites eschatology.org and bibleprophecy.com/.

Websites:

http://www.eschatology.org

http://www.bibleprophecy.com/

http://www.bereanbiblechurch.org/home.php

http://home.ad70.net/

http://www.fulfilledcg.com/Site/Magazine/magazine.htm

http://www.bibleprophecy.com/

http://www.asiteforthelord.com/id15.html

http://prophecydebate.com/

Books:

The Parousia by J. Stuart Russell

Before Jerusalem Fell by Kenneth Gentry

Avenging the Apostles and Prophets by Arthur M. Ogden

Essays on Eschatology by Sam Dawson

Last Days Madness by Gary Demar

Matthew 24 Fulfilled by John L. Bray

Exegetical Essays on the Resurrection by Sam Frost

Christianity's Great Dilemma by Glenn Hill

Behind the Veil of Moses by Brian Martin

The Cross and the Parousia of Christ by Max R. King

The Spirit of Prophecy by Max R. King

Like Father, Like Son, On Clouds of Glory by Don K. Preston

We Shall Meet Him in the Air by Don K. Preston

The Elements Shall Melt With Fervent Heat by Don K. Preston

Who Is This Babylon by Don K. Preston

The Last Days Identified by Don K. Preston

Into the World, Then Comes the End by Don K. Preston

70 Weeks Are Determined for the Resurrection by Don K. Preston

Seal Up Vision and Prophecy by Don K. Preston

Blast From the Past: The Truth About Armageddon by Don K. Preston